A Lenten Journey with *Jesus Christ* and St. Thérèse of Lisieux

An Invitation of Grace,

a Prayer of Hope,

and a Gift of Peace.

A LENTEN JOURNEY

with Jesus Christ and

ST. THÉRÈSE
OF LISIEUX

Daily Gospel Readings

with

Selections from the Writings

of

St. Thérèse of Lisieux

REFLECTIONS AND PRAYERS

BY

FR. JOHN F. RUSSELL, O. CARM.

WITH ADDITIONAL INTRODUCTORY MATERIAL BY

PETER J. MONGEAU

Christus
Publishing, LLC

WELLESLEY, MA
www.ChristusPublishing.com

Christus Publishing, LLC
Wellesley, Massachusetts
www.ChristusPublishing.com

Fr. John F. Russell, O.Carm. has been a Carmelite friar since 1954. He was ordained to the priesthood in 1960. He has earned several undergraduate and graduate degrees including a Licentiate in Sacred Theology (S.T.L.) at Lateran University in Rome and his Doctorate in Sacred Theology (S.T.D.) from Catholic University of America in 1979. Father Russell has had an association with Immaculate Conception Seminary, the graduate school of theology at Seton Hall University, for over twenty-two years, teaching Christian Anthropology and a variety of courses in Christian and Carmelite spirituality.

In the spring of 2009, Pope Benedict XVI awarded Father Russell the Benemerenti Medal for his exceptional service to the Catholic Church.

Peter J. Mongeau is the Founder and Publisher of Christus Publishing, LLC.

Publisher's Cataloging-in-Publication Data
Russell, John F., 1934-
    A Lenten Journey with Jesus Christ and St. Thérèse of Lisieux : daily Gospel readings with selections from the writings of St. Thérèse of Lisieux : reflections and prayers / by John F. Russell ; with additional introductory material by Peter J. Mongeau.
        p. ; cm.

    Includes bibliographical references.
    ISBN: 978-0-9841707-1-5

1. Lent--Prayers and devotions. 2. Thérèse, de Lisieux, Saint, 1873-1897.
3. Thérèse, de Lisieux, Saint, 1873-1897--Prayers and devotions. 4. Catholic Church--Prayers and devotions. 5. Carmelites--Prayers and devotions. 6. Prayer books. I. Mongeau Peter J. II. Title.

BX2170.L4 R87 2009
242/.34   2009938192

Printed and bound in the United State of America

10 9 8 7 6 5 4 3 2 1

Text design and layout by Peri Swan
This book was typeset in Garamond Premier Pro with Snell Roundhand as a display typeface

CONTENTS

ACKNOWLEDGMENTS

The Gospel passages are taken from the *Lectionary for Mass for Use in the Dioceses of the United States of America, second typical edition* © 2001, 1998, 1997, 1986, 1970, Confraternity of Christian Doctrine, Inc., Washington, DC. Used with permission. All rights reserved. No portion of this text may be reproduced by any means without permission in writing from the copyright owner.

The citations from St. Thérèse of Lisieux are from:

Story of a Soul, translated by John Clarke, O.C.D. Copyright (c) 1975, 1976, 1996 by Washington Province of Discalced Carmelites ICS Publications 2131 Lincoln Road, N.E., Washington, DC 20002-1199 U.S.A. www.icspublications.org

General Correspondence Volume Two translated by John Clarke, O.C.D. Copyright (c) 1988 by Washington Province of Discalced Carmelites ICS Publication 2131 Lincoln Road, N.E. Washington, DC 20002 U.S.A. www.icspublications.org

The Poetry of St. Therese of Lisieux translated by Donald Kinney, O.C.D.Copyright (c) 1995 by Washington Province of Discalced Carmelites ICS Publications 2131 Lincoln Road, N.E. Washington, DC 20002-1199 U.S.A. www.icspublications.org. Reprinted with permission.

Reflections and prayers copyright © 2009 Christus Publishing, LLC.

AN INVITATION
FROM
ST. THÉRÈSE
OF LISIEUX

Pope Pius X called St. Thérèse of Lisieux "the greatest saint of modern times." In 1997, Pope John Paul II declared her a Doctor of the Church for her spiritual wisdom inspired by the Gospel and her original theological insights and teaching. She is one of only three women to be declared a Doctor of the Church. She is commonly called the saint of "the Little Way" but her spirituality is much greater and deeper, for it is a path to our Lord God Jesus Christ—the Way, the Truth, and the Life.

St. Thérèse of Lisieux had a great love for God's Word, the Scriptures. In her own writings she employs the Old Testament over four hundred times and the New Testament over six hundred times. Scripture provided her with direction for her life as well as affirmation of her relationship to the Lord.

St. Thérèse wrote that the four Gospels were her greatest treasure. There she came to know Jesus Christ more profoundly and to love Him more deeply. She wrote, "I wanted *to love, to love Jesus with a passion,*

2

giving Him a thousand proofs of my love while it was possible. I copied out several passages on perfect love, on the reception God will give His Elect at the moment *He* becomes their Reward, great and eternal, and I repeated over and over the words of love burning in my heart" (*Story of a Soul,* 102–3).

The beautiful relationship that she had with Jesus can in some measure be ours. St. Thérèse invites us to join her in reflecting on God's Word in Lent, to allow God's Word to touch us in transforming ways. As we meet God's Word each day and join that Word to St. Thérèse's reflection, we will be drawn into prayer. The reflection provided for each day of Lent is meant to assist in moving into prayer and reflection. Our heart may wish to praise the Lord or simply to be thankful for all that we have received. We may find ourselves resting with a word or a phrase over a period of time because the word engages our heart.

Our prayerful mindfulness of a word or a phrase is truly a form of *lectio divina,* an ancient form of prayer in which God's Word is central. The experience of God's Word in *lectio* is life giving, providing a way of bonding with God's love.

St. Thérèse invites us to sit or to kneel and to put ourselves in the presence of God. God is always with us but we need to become mindful of His loving presence within us. From that act of faith, we can begin our Lenten meditation. Ask St. Thérèse to accompany you and to help you to draw closer to the living God Who is Christ Jesus, the Lord.

Fr. John F. Russell, O. Carm.

ST. THÉRÈSE
OF LISIEUX:
A SHORT
BIOGRAPHY

St. Thérèse of Lisieux was born Marie Françoise Thérèse Martin on January 2, 1873 in Alençon (Normandy) France. She was baptized two days later at the parish Church of Notre Dame. Because her mother was ill with breast cancer, Thérèse was sent to live with a wet nurse, Rose Taillé, who lived a few miles away. For a little over a year, Thérèse was cared for by Rose and indeed bonded with her to some degree. When she returned home in April of 1874, she had to adjust to her family and in particular to her mother. In fact, her mother, Blessed Zelie, schooled Thérèse in the ways of faith and formed her early on in the spiritual life. In the nineteenth century, Catholic France had adopted a reparative form of piety.

In her autobiography, *Story of a Soul,* Thérèse divides her life into three periods: (1) her birth until the death of her mother (1873–1877); (2) her years in the Benedictine Abbey School in Lisieux (1881–1886), a rather distressing time; and (3) her time at Carmel.

Thérèse's difficulties began when she was placed in a class with girls more advanced in age than Thérèse. She had to face the taunts of older girls and one teenager was particularly hard on Thérèse. Thérèse almost always received the higher grades in the class and thus provoked jealousy in many of the students. Thérèse suffered because she was quite timid and sensitive and cried easily. Her extreme sensitivity showed itself when her "second mother," her sister Pauline, went off to Carmel in 1882. It appears that Thérèse suffered a breakdown lasting a couple of months. No doctor knew what to do with her. Her family placed a statue of her mother's (she had died in August of 1877), Our Lady of Victories, by Thérèse's bedside and one day as Thérèse gazed upon the statue she sensed that Our Lady smiled at her. The point is that Thérèse recovered rather quickly and moved on with her life.

It was Christmas Eve of 1886 at midnight Mass that Thérèse experienced a conversion. It happened during her thanksgiving after communion. That night she claimed, "I felt charity enter my soul." The fact is that her penchant for crying at every perceived criticism left her. She was ready to deal with disappointments and difficulties more maturely.

On April 9, 1888, Thérèse entered Carmel and thus began the third and final period of her life. In May, she made a general confession to Father Pichon, who communicated to her that she had never committed a mortal sin. This set Thérèse on waves of confidence and peace. Eventually, all of the Martin girls entered religious life: Pauline, Marie, Thérèse, and Celine to the Carmelites, and Leonie, who became a religious with the Visitation nuns in Caen. On January 10, 1889, Thérèse received the Carmelite habit and began her novitiate. It was in this period that her father, Blessed Louis, was committed to Bon Sauveur Hospital in Caen. He did not return to Lisieux until 1892. Thérèse's sister Celine was home and became her father's caretaker. Blessed Louis did visit Carmel one more time, on May 12, 1892. He died in July of 1894.

On September 8, 1890, St. Thérèse made her profession of vows as a Carmelite. She reveals the story of her life and her spirituality in the *Story of a Soul*, a book containing three manuscripts that Thérèse composed at the request of her sisters. In 1895, she composed her first manuscript (A), which told the story of her early family life. It was written for her sister Pauline (Mother Agnes). The second manuscript (B) was written at the request of her sister Marie (Sister Marie of the Sacred Heart), who asked to have a souvenir of Thérèse's retreat (September 7–18, 1896). Manuscript B is a fine portrait of Thérèse's spirituality.

It needs to be said at the outset that St. Thérèse's spirituality is both theocentric and christocentric. Jesus is the love of her life. She sees her relationship to Him as well as to her Sisters in community as expressed in love. She discovered the importance of love in reading Scripture as well as the writings of St. John of the Cross. Since Thérèse did not think she had great gifts and was unable to practice grandiose mortification, she embraced her "little way." She could always provide a smile, a word of encouragement or a thoughtful affirmation; or she could offer a helping hand to her Sisters in the Carmel. She was careful not to judge others since she did not know the other's interior life. Yet, she is honest in declaring that she did not like everyone in the community. She rode above negative feelings and treated each one generously. She wrote that when she entered Carmel she was under no illusions. She knew that the life would require sacrifice. Consequently, she was a great gift to community life.

St. Thérèse loved prayer and rejoiced in leading the Divine Office. She enjoyed a lively faith, except in the last year or so of her life. Her story reveals a strong accent on hope, and love, of course, led her toward the eternal shore, as she would say. She volunteered to assist the nun in the laundry room when no one else would volunteer. She consistently assisted an elderly nun who was cranky and difficult to serve. There was nothing extraordinary in her service so it seems, but she lived always a life of integrity and virtue. A number of the nuns she lived with did not see anything extraordinary about her life. One asked, When she dies what shall be written about her? She came here, she lived here, and she died here.

St. Thérèse served the community as an assistant novice mistress. In fact, her sister Celine was one of her novices. Several novices noted in testimony at the diocesan process for beatification and canonization that St. Thérèse had a marvelous grasp of Scriptural passages. When she spoke God's Word came alive.

The two volumes of *General Correspondence* (herein *The Letters of St. Thérèse*) contain letters St. Thérèse received and wrote to two "spiritual brothers": Fr. Maurice Bellière, a seminarian who was ordained and served for several years as a missionary in Africa and Fr. Adolphe Roulland of the Foreign Missions in Paris, who served in China. He said one of his first Masses at Carmel in Lisieux. A study of the correspondence between Maurice Bellière and St. Thérèse is engaging reading, entitled *Maurice and Thérèse: The Story of a Love*, it reveals the human touch of St. Thérèse (see Suggestions for Further Reading).

It was during the Triduum of Holy Week in 1896, that Thérèse had the first indication of her tuberculosis. She suffered from the illness for a little more than one year. In the nineteenth century, there was no cure for the illness. Death came ultimately by slow asphyxiation. At approximately the same time tuberculosis set in, she also began to experience powerful temptations against the existence of heaven. She describes it as a period of darkness and doubt. At times, she would experience some relief but the temptation would return with greater darkness than before. The temptation never left her. St. Thérèse's darkness bears a strong resemblance to the darkness that Blessed Teresa of Calcutta met in her life. But in both cases there seems to be a joy and a peace at a deeper level of their lives and they each faithfully continued to live out the vocation to which they were called.

St. Thérèse became deathly ill in April of 1897. At this time, her blood sisters began to write down Thérèse's last words. Yet she still had the strength to write manuscript C of *Story of a Soul*, which are her thoughts on life at Carmel of Lisieux. Eventually, the three manuscripts (A, B, and C) became the one volume, *Story of a Soul*.

On July 8, 1897, St. Thérèse was moved to the infirmary of the monastery, which was on the first floor. She continued to write her autobiography and completed manuscript C. On July 30, 1897, she was anointed; on August 19 of the same year, she received Communion for the last time. After an agony that lasted two days, St. Thérèse died on September 30 at 7:30 p.m. Her burial in the Lisieux cemetery took place on October 4, 1897.

It is interesting to note that St. Thérèse rose above the religious culture of her time, which was centered on the image of God as Divine Justice. Yet St. Thérèse along with her sister Celine (Sister Genviève) made acts of oblation to Merciful Love. In contrast to the sense of fear that was pervasive in French spirituality St. Thérèse asked, "How could anyone be afraid of a God who became a child?" Living in a period when Jansenism[1] still had a hold on French spirituality, St. Thérèse promoted frequent communion. She commented, "I don't think God came among us simply to remain in a ciborium. Rather he wants the ciborium of our hearts."

St. Thérèse was canonized by Pope Pius XI on May 17, 1925. She was proclaimed the Universal Patron of the Missions, with St. Francis Xavier, on December 14, 1927. Pope John Paul II declared her a Doctor of the Church on October 19, 1997. St. Thérèse is one of the top two most popular saints in the Church, sharing the honor with St. Francis of Assisi. *Story of a Soul* has been translated into over fifty languages and dialects. Her popularity seems to rest on the fact that she puts the call to holiness within the reach of ordinary people.

The Institute for Carmelite Studies and ICS Publications is located in Washington, D.C. All of St. Thérèse's writings are published there. *Story of a Soul*, translated by John Clarke, O.C.D., is available in its third edition. Also available are the two volumes of her *General Correspondence*, her *Prayers*, her *Poetry*, translated by Donald Kinney, O.C.D., and *The Plays of St. Thérèse of Lisieux*, translated by Susan Conroy and David Dwyer.

FR. JOHN F. RUSSELL, O. CARM.

---

1. Jansenism is a movement begun by Cornelius Jansen (1585-1638) in France. It was a form of stern asceticism which arose from a very pessimistic view of humanity. While the movement was condemned by the Church its influence lingered into the twentieth century. The movement opposed frequent communion, for example, because frequent communion encouraged laxity towards confession.

THE CARMELITE
ORDER:
AN OVERVIEW

The Carmelite Order traces its beginnings to the early thirteenth century when a community living in discipleship of Jesus Christ as hermits on Mount Carmel sought ecclesiastical approval. Albert, Patriarch of Jerusalem, provided the first Carmelites with a Rule, which he gave sometime between 1209 and 1214. The Rule is brief (eighteen paragraphs), simple, and flexible. The Rule is christocentric, calls for simplicity of life (everything held in common), and encourages daily gathering for the celebration of the Eucharist. At that time, the oratory, located in the center of the monastic cells at Carmel, was dedicated to Our Lady. Typically, the monks remained in their cells, meditating day and night on the law of the Lord, unless occupied in other just works. The original Rule of St. Albert of Jerusalem was addressed to Brother B. and the other hermits. Since we do not know who Brother B. was, Carmelites cannot claim a particular founder like a Francis or a Dominic.

The Turkish invasions of the Holy Land in the thirteenth century threatened the Carmelites who had to migrate to Europe in 1238 and 1241, discovering along the way that they could not retain their hermitic way of life. The earliest extant copy of the Carmelite Constitutions (1281) indicates that the hermits shifted to a mendicant form of religious life, similar to the Franciscans and the Dominicans. Mendicants lived as beggars among the poor and serving the poor in a variety of ways. Even with the change to a cenobitic or communal form of life, the Carmelites continued to value silence, prayer, and recollection. Thus in 1247, Pope Innocent IV made changes to the Carmelite Rule, which enabled the Carmelites to live as a mendicant community in Europe and elsewhere.

Early on, the Carmelite Order claimed a special relationship to Mary, the Mother of God. In fact, as noted, the oratory at Mt. Carmel was dedicated to Mary. The original name for the Carmelites is "the brothers of the Blessed Virgin Mary." Carmelites also take Elijah as a model for the religious life.

Elijah has always had a special role in monastic history because he sought the face of God, he was steeped in the religious tradition of Israel, and he was creative in the face of adversity. Elijah defended the true worship of Yahweh and slew the false prophets of Baal after Ahab, the king of Israel, married Jezebel, princess of Tyre. Jezebel did not share the religious background of Israel and sought to have Israel conform to the worship of Baal. Baalism had many prophets who stood in opposition to the Israelite tradition. Elijah opposed Jezebel, in part, because he had an intimacy with God, which is the product of a prayerful heart. Carmelites respect Elijah's fidelity to God in the midst of adversity.

Many men and women of Carmel not only represent the best of the Carmelite heritage but also have enriched the life of the Church. Perhaps best known in the mystical tradition are St. Teresa of Avila and St. John of the Cross. St. Teresa initiated reform in Carmel (reform always seeks to return to the purity of the Gospel) and eventually the reform became a new community in Carmel: the Discalced Carmelites.

St. Teresa is known for her writings on prayer. Her use of images of water and rooms of the interior castle are certainly enlightening. St. John of the Cross offers a view of growth in the interior life through his analysis of the process of purification. His image of the dark night of the soul sheds light on the nature of the inner life. Other writings that assist in grasping the nature of spiritual life are the works of St. Thérèse of Lisieux and Blessed Elizabeth of the Trinity.

It should be noted that the Teresian reform was not the only reform movement. There was reform in Mantua in Italy and in the seventeenth century, the Carmelite Reform of Touraine. The latter reform created a treatise on prayer to be used by candidates entering the Order. The practice of the presence of God was expounded in that reform. In fact, mindfulness of God has always held an important place in Carmelite life.

Carmelites have never identified one ministry as peculiar to Carmel. Carmelites are in education, parish ministry, spiritual centers and retreat houses, and serve as chaplains in hospitals and prisons. What is important always is immersion in the life of prayer.

We can sum up the Carmelite spirituality in the following ways:

- Practice of the Presence of God
- Focus on God's Word in *lectio divina*
- Commitment to the liturgical and sacramental life of the Church
- Mary, the model of contemplative prayer and Elijah, the father of the contemplative spirit
- Emphasis on the affective dimension of prayer
- Service of God's people, especially those in most need
- Commitment to discipleship of Jesus Christ and to growth in the virtues of faith, hope, and love
- Confidence and hope in God's merciful love

In the present day, Carmelites live and practice throughout the world with foundations in the Americas, the Caribbean, Europe, Asia, and Africa.   The Constitution of the Order (voted in 1995) supports members in their efforts to help people in their search for God and their life of prayer. This seems particularly important at a time when the atheism of forgetfulness of God is a strong force in the world.

FR. JOHN F. RUSSELL, O. CARM.

THE
LENTEN
SEASON

Dear Brothers and Sisters!

Once again, the Lord is calling us to follow him along the journey of Lent. Each year all the faithful are invited to respond anew as individuals and as a community to our baptismal vocation and to bear fruits of conversion. Lent is a journey of evolving, creative reflection which inspires penance and gives new impetus to every aspect of our commitment to follow the Gospel. It is a journey of love which opens the hearts of believers to our brothers and sisters and draws them to God. Jesus asks his disciples to live and to radiate charity.

JOHN PAUL II, MESSAGE FOR LENT 1996

In the Carmelite Orders of France in the nineteenth century, Lent was a period devoted to self-abnegation as a way of preparing the heart for a deeper commitment to Christ. Prayer and fasting, silence and solitude, devotion to the Passion of Christ shaped the Lenten devotion. The nuns did no letter writing in this period until the celebration of Easter. St. Thérèse once said, "it was not through letters Carmelites must save souls but through prayer" (*Story of a Soul,* 241).

Vatican Council II focused on two aspects of Lent. In the Constitution on the Sacred Liturgy we read, "The two elements which are especially characteristic of Lent—the recalling of baptism or the preparation for it, and penance—should be given greater emphasis in the liturgy and in liturgical catechesis. It is by means of them that the Church prepares the faithful for the celebration of Easter, while they hear God's Word more frequently and devote more time to prayer"(no. 109).

One can see the contrast between the two views of Lent. In nineteenth-century France, the Lenten focus was on asceticism. Vatican II ties Lent to the sacrament of baptism since baptism is the foundation of spiritual life and therefore, the true preparation for Lent.

While a Lenten period of at least some days was celebrated in the early Church, Lent did not achieve the status of a forty-day fast until the fourth century. To abstain from meat was a common form of fasting. Also, there arose the practice of giving up something good as a way to develop spiritual muscle. However, the most important practice in the Lenten period is to focus upon Christ who gave His life for us. The life, death, and Resurrection of Jesus are the life blood of the Lenten period. The true fast of Lent is to turn away from deliberate sin in order genuinely to cultivate the virtuous life. Sanctity is the call of the Christian from the day of baptism. Lent helps us to keep the goal before us.

FR. JOHN F. RUSSELL, O. CARM.

PRAYER, SCRIPTURE, AND *LECTIO DIVINA*

According to St. John Damascene, prayer is "the raising of one's mind and heart to God or the request of good things from God" (*De Fide Orth*. 3, 24: PG 94, 1089C). Prayer is the most fundamental response we give to God's love for us. Prayer is always grounded in faith. Section Four of the Catholic Catechism provides a marvelous synthesis of the meaning of prayer.

In Scripture, there are many examples of prayer. The humble prayer of Abraham is evident in Genesis 15:1-6. Moses' prayer reveals a solid intimacy with God in Exodus 34:6. First Samuel 3:9–10 tells of Samuel's encounter with God. Elijah the prophet sought God's intercession so that he might become strong in First Kings 18:39. The Psalms express the prayer of God's people gathered in the Temple.

Jesus manifests an engaging sense of intimacy with His Father: he withdrew from the demands of ministry to spend an evening in prayer and went out into the desert to pray; He prayed before His

Transfiguration and He prayed before choosing the twelve apostles. When asked, He taught his disciples the "Our Father."

In the Christian tradition, prayer expresses praise of God. The Eucharistic prayer is thanksgiving. Petition for our needs and sorrow over sin are also expressions of authentic prayer.

Prayer can be vocal, meditative, or contemplative. Vocal prayer involves words, whether vocal or mental, issuing from the heart. Jesus taught his disciples the "Our Father," which is vocal prayer. Vocal prayer begins contemplative prayer.

Meditation is a form of prayer that engages our thoughts, imagination, and desires. Meditation occurs as we reflect on what we have read from Scripture or from a Christian classic such as St. Thérèse's *Story of a Soul*. In meditation, we focus on the mysteries of Christ to deepen our conversion and commitment to Christ. In *lectio divina*, we attend to God's Word so that our daily life can be shaped by the internalized Word of God.

Finally, there is contemplative prayer in which our attention centers on Jesus who is with us. As the Catholic Catechism states, "Contemplation is a gaze of faith, fixed on Jesus" (no. 2715). So, contemplation dwells in the love of God. The recollection of the heart touches all forms of prayer.

Liturgical prayer communicates the mystery of salvation, God's great gift and blessing to us in Christ Jesus.

The struggles in prayer include distractions or discouragement when our prayer is dry. Our mission is to trust in God's presence and love for us. Again, the foundation of all prayer is faith.

LECTIO DIVINA

ON SEPTEMBER 16, 2005 POPE BENEDICT XVI SAID,

I would like in particular to recall and recommend the ancient tradition of lectio divina: "the diligent reading of Sacred Scripture accompanied by prayer brings about that intimate dialogue in which the person read-

ing hears God who is speaking, and in praying, responds to him with trusting openness of heart" (cf. *Dei Verbum,* n. 25). *If it is effectively promoted, this practice will bring to the Church—I am convinced of it—a new spiritual springtime.*

Lectio divina is the ancient tradition of praying with Scripture so that the Word of God infuses us so that we may grow closer to God and His love. *Lectio divina* in Latin means divine reading or holy reading; many once practiced this form of prayer but today *lectio divina* is used primarily in monastic communities and by those who have adapted some forms of monastic spirituality in their daily lives.

    Lectio divina has four stages. *Lectio* (reading), where we read the Word of God slowly, prayerfully, and try to immerse ourselves in the Word of God. The second stage is *meditatio* (meditate), when we meditate on a phrase or passage of Scripture we have read. The third stage is *oratio* (prayer or dialogue), when we pray to God with our present urgings or longings for God. The final stage is *comtemplatio* (contemplation), when we simply place ourselves in the presence of God and love God.

    With this book, you will have the opportunity to deepen your spiritual life and practice the many forms of prayer including *lectio divina.* May you try all the forms of prayer, and may God lead you to his holiness. Prayer life is a rewarding life, but it may take more effort than we are prepared to undertake. Persevere. Some days our prayers will be easy, other days hard or unfulfilling. Persevere. We may have distractions: work, home life, or illness. Persevere. Some days we are reminded of our sins and see ourselves and all our flaws. Persevere. As we move closer to God, His light will shine on us—and we will see our imperfections reflected against His perfect Love. Persevere. His light will envelope us and His Love will grant us His Peace.

FR. JOHN F. RUSSELL, O.CARM

PETER J. MONGEAU

ST. THÉRÈSE
OF LISIEUX
ON PRAYER

As a Carmelite, St. Thérèse was committed to several hours of prayer each day. Some of the time was spent in communal prayer with the recitation of the Divine Office in choir, that is, in the chapel of the monastery. In fact, St. Thérèse wrote that she "loved very much the prayers in common, for Jesus has promised to be in the midst of those who gather together in His name" (*Story of a Soul*, 242).

At Carmel, two hours each day were devoted to silent prayer or meditation. St. Thérèse put great confidence in the efficacy of prayer. "I do like children who do not know how to read; I say very simply to God what I wish to say, without composing beautiful sentences and He always understands me" (ibid., 242).

St. Thérèse never produced a method of prayer, yet her description of prayer was chosen for the Universal Catholic Catechism. "For me, prayer is an aspiration of the heart, it is a simple glance directed to heaven, it is a cry of gratitude and love in the midst of trial as well as joy; finally it is something great, supernatural, which expands my soul and unites me to Jesus" (ibid., 242).

As a child, St. Thérèse wrote about her meditation on the morning of her first visit to the Carmel of Lisieux after Pauline's entrance. "The morning of the day I was to visit, I was thinking over in my bed (for it was there I made my profound meditations), and contrary to the Bride in the Canticles, I always found my Beloved there" (ibid., 71). Particularly helpful for prayer to St. Thérèse were the Gospels and *The Imitation of Christ* by Thomas à Kempis. Meditation on these writings always stirred her heart.

Did St. Thérèse have to face distractions in prayer? Or, the lack of consolation? It certainly seems so. "Sometimes when my mind is in such great aridity that it is impossible to draw forth one single thought to unite me with God, I very slowly recite an Our Father and then the angelic salutation; then these prayers give me great delight, they nourish my soul much more than if I had recited them precipitately a hundred times" (ibid., 243).

St. Thérèse admitted that the recitation of the rosary "is more difficult for me than the wearing of an instrument of penance" (ibid., 242). She had a difficult time focusing on the mysteries of the rosary. Still, she had a solid devotion to Mary as her mother and St. Thérèse felt Mary's protection in her life.

St. Thérèse meditated with the Gospel or *Imitation* in her hands. This seems apparent from a comment she made regarding a Sister in front of her in choir. This Sister must have had "many lights because she rarely used a book during meditation" (ibid., 249). St. Thérèse would use the Gospels to stir her imagination and to move her heart with sentiments of love or thanksgiving to Jesus.

St. Thérèse stands in the Carmelite tradition of valuing prayer as communion with God. Jesus was her Beloved and prayer is always time spent with Him. Moreover, her prayer life had further goals throughout her life: to save sinners and to assist the ministry of priests.

We understand prayer best in the writings of St. Thérèse as a fundamental way of being with God. She was mindful of God's presence in her life each day, calling her to spend her life in service to God and to others. She experienced the unity of love for God and love for others. She viewed love in the traditional Gospel sense of willing the good of another. She recognized that love is costly but she was willing to embrace the Cross as a manifestation of union with Jesus Christ.

Fr. John F. Russell, O. Carm.

ON THE DAILY GOSPEL READINGS

As noted, this book presents daily readings and prayers for every day of Lent, weekdays, and Sundays. The daily readings begin with a Gospel Reading, followed by a quote from St. Thérèse's writings, a reflection, and a prayer.

The Gospel Readings are from the Roman Catholic *Lectionary for Mass for Use in the Dioceses of the United States of America.* The *Lectionary for Mass* contains the readings for Mass selected from the Bible.

If you were to attend daily Mass during Lent in the United States, you would hear the same Daily Gospel Readings included in this book. For example, the Ash Wednesday Gospel Reading, Matthew 6:1–6, 16–18, is the same Gospel Reading you would hear when you attend Mass to receive your ashes. In fact, on each day at all the Masses of the Latin-rite Roman Catholic Church throughout the world, the same readings are heard in Mass, read in the vernacular language or Latin.

There are two main components of the Lectionary: Sunday and Weekday readings. Sunday readings are arranged on a three-year cycle: Year A, Year B, and Year C. The Gospel Readings for Year A are generally from the Gospel of St. Matthew, Year B are generally from the Gospel of St. Mark, and Year C are generally from the Gospel of St. Luke. St. John's Gospel is read on Sundays in Year A, B, and C during specific liturgical calendar periods.

The Weekday readings are on a two-year cycle: Year I and Year II. Year I are odd-numbered years and Year II are even-numbered years. The Weekday readings during Lent are the same for Year I and Year II but differ each day. In this book, the Weekday Gospel Readings are also the Weekday Gospel Readings in the Lectionary.

For Sundays, you have three different selections of readings and prayers. Each selection begins with a different Gospel Reading, the Gospel Reading from Year A, B, or C of the Lectionary.

Appendix A, the Calendar for Lent 2010–2019 & Lectionary Cycle, lists the specific dates for the next ten years for Ash Wednesday, the Sundays of Lent, and includes the Sunday Lectionary Cycle for the year. Please refer to the table to determine the current year's Sunday Lectionary Cycle: Year A, B, or C and select the appropriate Sunday reading for the present year.

This book in a small way invites you to pray each day with the Church and your fellow Christians in the world on your Lenten journey with Jesus Christ and St. Thérèse.

PETER J. MONGEAU

"I understand and I know from experience that: *'The kingdom of God is within you.'* Jesus has no need of books or teachers to instruct souls; He teaches without the noise of words. Never have I heard Him speak, but I feel that He is within me at each moment; He is guiding and inspiring me with what I must say and do. I find just when I need them certain lights that I had not seen until then, and it isn't most frequently during my hours of prayer that these are most abundant but rather in the midst of my daily occupations"(*Story of a Soul,* 179).

ST. THÉRÈSE OF LISIEUX

ASH
WEDNESDAY
*and the Days
after Ash Wednesday*

GOSPEL

JESUS SAID TO HIS DISCIPLES:

"Take care not to perform righteous deeds in order that people may see them; otherwise, you will have no recompense from your heavenly Father. When you give alms, do not blow a trumpet before you, as the hypocrites do in the synagogues and in the streets to win the praise of others. Amen, I say to you, they have received their reward. But when you give alms, do not let your left hand know what your right is doing, so that your almsgiving may be secret. And your Father who sees in secret will repay you.

"When you pray, do not be like the hypocrites, who love to stand and pray in the synagogues and on street corners so that others may see them. Amen, I say to you, they have received their reward. But when you pray, go to your inner room, close the door, and pray to your Father in secret. And your Father who sees in secret will repay you.

"When you fast, do not look gloomy like the hypocrites. They neglect their appearance, so that they may appear to others to be fasting. Amen, I say to you, they have received their reward. But when you fast, anoint your head and wash your face, so that you may not appear to be fasting, except to your Father who is hidden. And your Father who sees what is hidden will repay you."

MATTHEW 6: 1-6, 16-18

ST. THÉRÈSE OF LISIEUX

"And so it is in the world of souls, Jesus' garden. He willed to create great souls comparable to Lilies and roses, but he has created smaller ones and these must be content to be daisies or violets destined to give joy to God's glances when he looks down at his feet. Perfection consists in doing His will, in being what he wills us to be" (Story of a Soul, 14).[1]

REFLECTION

St. Thérèse believed in the value of the hidden life. She knew that sincere commitment to a life of faith, hope, and love in Jesus Christ would serve to help bring about new life in others. She gave her life for the conversion of sinners and for priests. The pride and self-centeredness revealed in today's Gospel had no echo in St. Thérèse's life. St. Thérèse was totally Christ-centered and thus modeled Christ's self-emptying love. She liked to view herself as a little flower, unexceptional, yet embraced by God's merciful love.

PRAYER

Lord, our God, guard our hearts from the ways of arrogance and pride. Help us in this Lenten season to follow Jesus with sincere hearts and humble lives. May we manifest the integrity that marks the life of St. Thérèse. We make our prayer through Christ our Lord.

---

1. The quotation is from St. Thérèse in *Story of a Soul: The Autobiography of St. Thérèse of Lisieux,* 3rd ed., trans. from the original manuscripts by John Clarke, O.C.D. (Washington, DC: ICS Publications, 1996). Hereafter, *Story of a Soul.*

GOSPEL

JESUS SAID TO HIS DISCIPLES:

"The Son of Man must suffer greatly and be rejected by the elders, the chief priests, and the scribes, and be killed and on the third day be raised."

Then he said to all, "If anyone wishes to come after me, he must deny himself and take up his cross daily and follow me. For whoever wishes to save his life will lose it, but whoever loses his life for my sake will save it. What profit is there for one to gain the whole world yet lose or forfeit himself?"

LUKE 9: 22-25

ST. THÉRÈSE OF LISIEUX

"On New Year's day, 1888, Jesus again gave me a present of his cross, but this time I was alone in carrying it. It was all the more painful as I did not understand it. A letter from Mother Marie de Gonzague informed me that the Bishop's answer had arrived December 28, feast of the Holy Innocents, but that she had not told me as it was decided that my entrance would be delayed until after Lent. I was unable to hold back my tears at the thought of such a long wait I really want to believe I must have appeared unreasonable in not accepting my three months exile joyfully, but I also believe that, without its appearing so, this trial was very great and made me grow very much in abandonment and in the other virtues" (Story of a Soul, 143).

REFLECTION

The cross enters everyone's life and we notice in today's Gospel reading that the cross is a daily event. For St. Thérèse the cross was experienced in the delay she had to endure before her entrance into the Carmel of Lisieux. She would encounter more crosses in her brief life, e.g., physical illness and temptations regarding the existence of heaven.

People meet the cross in disappointments with children, in job loss and financial crises. Also the cross comes in the form of a migraine headache, in risky surgery, in stress, in long waiting lines, in dryness in prayer, in rejection in relationships. The cross may be brief and transitory or permanent. It may be simply an annoyance or a dark period in one's life which threatens one's overall mental health. In the Christian tradition we walk in the footsteps of Christ, who can take our suffering and turn it into a saving grace for others. We may find that our desire to unite with Christ and his suffering provides us with the ballast of peace and hope. For St. Thérèse suffering provided the joy of knowing Christ Jesus in profound love.

PRAYER

Gracious and loving God, your presence among us invites courage and fidelity in adversity. Suffering can cause feelings of anger and pain as well as a heart that may question your goodness. Take our lives and transform our hearts to trust in your love and your presence within us. Like St. Thérèse may we obtain the grace of abandonment to your providential love. We make our prayer through Christ our Lord. Amen.

GOSPEL

The disciples of John approached Jesus and said, "Why do we and the Pharisees fast much, but your disciples do not fast?" Jesus answered them, "Can the wedding guests mourn as long as the bridegroom is with them? The days will come when the bridegroom is taken away from them, and then they will fast."

MATTHEW 9: 14-15

ST. THÉRÈSE OF LISIEUX

"Jesus, you are the Lamb I love,
You are all I need, O supreme good!
In you I have everything, the earth and even Heaven.
The Flower that I pick, O my King!
Is You!"

(Excerpted from the poem, *"He Who has Jesus has Everything"* in *The Poetry of St. Thérèse,* 104).[1]

---

2. *The Poetry of St. Thérèse of Lisieux,* trans. Donald Kenney, O.C.D. (Washington, DC, ICS Publications, 1996). Hereafter, *The Poetry of St. Thérèse.*

REFLECTION

Fasting is part of the ascetical tradition of religions generally. In Christianity it is meant to be a tool to serve moderation in food and drink and so to discipline desires. The Carmel of Lisieux took part in rituals of fasting, particularly but not exclusively during Lent. St. Thérèse shared in that discipline. Her poem demonstrates that the goal of the Christian life and of all discipline is to come to know and to love Jesus Christ. "In You I have everything" writes St. Thérèse.

The fasting which we take on in Lent should not be viewed apart from our relationship to Jesus Christ. To come to know and to love Jesus is the goal of our lives. Prayer, fasting, penance, almsgiving are all expressions of the heart's desire: to walk with the Lord in integrity of life.

PRAYER

Merciful Father, help us to follow the discipline of Lent. Let us fast from all that would compromise our relationship to you. Like St. Thérèse enable us to be faithful in following you, to be generous in our relationship to others and to manifest a forgiving heart. We make our prayer through Christ our Lord. Amen.

GOSPEL

Jesus saw a tax collector named Levi sitting at the customs post. He said to him, "Follow me." And leaving everything behind, he got up and followed him. Then Levi gave a great banquet for him in his house, and a large crowd of tax collectors and others were at table with them. The Pharisees and their scribes complained to his disciples, saying, "Why do you eat and drink with tax collectors and sinners?" Jesus said to them in reply, "Those who are healthy do not need a physician, but the sick do. I have not come to call the righteous to repentance but sinners."

LUKE 5: 27-32

ST. THÉRÈSE OF LISIEUX

"More merciful to me than He was to His disciples, Jesus took the net Himself *and cast it, and drew it in filled with fish. He made me a fisher of* souls. *I experienced a great desire to work for the conversion of sinners, a desire I hadn't felt so intensely before" (Story of a Soul, 99).*

REFLECTION

Jesus came to call sinners to conversion and to a life of faith, hope and love. As St. Thérèse draws closer to the Lord she experiences a call within her vocation to Carmel . . . to work for the conversion of sinners. Her daily commitment to prayer, to community life and her openness to suffering became a lifestyle offered in love to Jesus for the sake of sinners.

In the Lenten season we can put confidence in God's merciful love toward each one of us. We need not ever be captive of discouragement. Lent provides us with an opportunity to approach the sacrament of Penance and reconciliation. It is a sacrament in which God's merciful love and forgiveness can be received. What a grace it is to walk in newness of life!

PRAYER

Loving Father, we give you praise and thank you for your great love for us. Give us the wisdom to recognize the many ways in which your mercy is present in our lives. May we have the grace to accept the call to a deeper conversion and to conform our lives in discipleship of Jesus. Amen.

FIRST WEEK
OF
LENT

GOSPEL

At that time Jesus was led by the Spirit into the desert to be tempted by the devil. He fasted for forty days and forty nights, and afterwards he was hungry. The tempter approached and said to him, "If you are the Son of God, command that these stones become loaves of bread."

He said in reply, "It is written: / *One does not live on bread alone, / but on every word that comes forth from the mouth of God."* / Then the devil took him to the holy city, and made him stand on the parapet of the temple, and said to him, "If you are the Son of God, throw yourself down. For it is written: / *He will command his angels concerning you / and with their hands they will support you, / lest you dash your foot against a stone."* / Jesus answered him, "Again it is written, *You shall not put the Lord, your God, to the test."* Then the devil took him up to a very high mountain, and showed him all the kingdoms of the world in their magnificence, and he said to him, "All these I shall give to you, if you will prostrate yourself and worship me." At this, Jesus said to him, "Get away, Satan! It is written: / *The Lord, your God, shall you worship / and him alone shall you serve."* / Then the devil left him and, behold, angels came and ministered to him.

MATTHEW 4: 1-11

ST. THÉRÈSE OF LISIEUX

"Dear Mother [Mother Marie de Gonzague, Prioress]*, you are the compass Jesus has given me as a sure guide to the eternal shore. How sweet it is to fix my eyes upon you and thus accomplish the will of the Lord! Since the time He permitted me to suffer temptations against* faith, *He has greatly increased the* spirit of faith *in my heart"* (Story of a Soul, *219).*

36

REFLECTION

The confrontation between Jesus and Satan is a test of strength. At a deeper level of meaning we have a clash between the Kingdom of God and the kingdom of Satan. Here the word of God confronts the power of evil. Jesus offers us a model for resisting temptation, rooted in his confidence in the truth of God's word. Jesus acts decisively and God's word sustains him. Recently, in a homily for the first Sunday in Lent, Pope Benedict noted that angels ministered to Jesus and they can help to strengthen us in following Jesus Christ.

St. Thérèse suffered from temptations against faith, in particular regarding the existence of heaven. She claims that she made more acts of faith during the time of temptation that at any other time in her life. She never wavered in trusting in God's love for her.

Temptation is usually alluring; it certainly was to Adam and Eve. Temptation seeks to draw us into a world of gratification, but the outcome is never one of peace. Lent reminds us that our focus is on coming to know and to love Jesus Christ. Jesus will lead us to a self-emptying love for others. This is the path to fulfillment. The Church, which is the Body of Christ, gives us courage and strength, in particular through the gift of the Eucharist.

PRAYER

God of all creation, help each one of us to resist the attractions of evil and sin. We need your grace in order to live by the truth of your Word. Help us to be faithful in the ordinary and the everyday. We make our prayer through Christ our Lord. Amen.

GOSPEL

The Spirit drove Jesus out into the desert, and he remained in the desert for forty days, tempted by Satan. He was among wild beasts, and the angels ministered to him.

After John had been arrested, Jesus came to Galilee proclaiming the gospel of God: "This the time of fulfillment. The kingdom of God is at hand. Repent, and believe in the gospel."

MARK 1: 12-15

ST. THÉRÈSE OF LISIEUX

"I understand and I know from experience that: 'The kingdom of God is within you' [Luke 17:2]. Jesus has no need of books or teachers to instruct souls; He teaches without the noise of words. Never have I heard Him speak, but I feel He is within me at each moment; He is guiding and inspiring me with what I must say and do" (Story of a Soul, 179).

REFLECTION

The Gospel of Mark does not provide the detail we find in Matthew and Luke regarding Jesus' temptations in the desert. We know the outcome: Jesus is victorious over Satan. What is highlighted in this Gospel is Jesus' word in Galilee: "The kingdom of God is at hand. Repent and believe in the Gospel."

St. Thérèse envisions the kingdom within her, which reminds us of the truth of the indwelling Trinity in our lives as the result of our baptism. It is Jesus who directs and inspires St. Thérèse regarding what she is to say and to do. St. Thérèse was certainly mindful of God in the everyday. She was alert to grace moving her in the ways of love.

Lent gives us opportunity to recognize how God is at work in us. Obviously, God's grace would have us resist temptation to sin, follow the impulse to be patient and forgiving, and cultivate a sense of the presence of God in our lives through faith.

PRAYER

God of all consolation, strengthen us to resist the power of evil and to place our trust in you always. May a sacramental life lead us to rejoice that God is with us and that His kingdom is reflected in the liturgy and in the life of the Church. We make our prayer through Christ our Lord. Amen.

GOSPEL

Filled with the Holy Spirit, Jesus returned from the Jordan and was led by the Spirit into the desert for forty days, to be tempted by the devil. He ate nothing during those days, and when they were over he was hungry. The devil said to him, "If you are the Son of God, command this stone to become bread." Jesus answered him, "It is written, *One does not live on bread alone.*" Then he took him up and showed him all the kingdoms of the world in a single instant. The devil said to him, "I shall give to you all this power and glory; for it has been handed over to me, and I may give it to whomever I wish. All this will be yours, if you worship me." Jesus said to him in reply, "It is written: / *You shall worship the Lord, your God, and him alone shall you serve.*" / Then he led them to Jerusalem, made him stand on the parapet of the temple, and said to him, "If you are the Son of God, throw yourself down from here, for it is written: / *He will command his angels concerning you, to guard you,* / and: / *With their hands they will support you,* / *lest you dash your foot against a stone.*" / Jesus said to him in reply, "It also says, *You shall not put the Lord, your God, to the test.*" When the devil had finished every temptation, he departed from him for a time.

LUKE 4: 1-13

ST. THÉRÈSE OF LISIEUX

St. Thérèse quotes from Psalm 118, *"I have had understanding above old men, because I have sought your will. Your word is a lamp to my feet. I am prepared to carry out your commandments and I am TROUBLED ABOUT NOTHING."* She adds, *"You did not hesitate, dear Mother* [Mother Marie de Gonsague, Prioress], *to tell me one day that God was enlightening my soul and that he was giving me even the experience of* years" *(Story of a Soul,* 209–10).

REFLECTION

Jesus says in St. Luke's Gospel that one does not live on bread alone. St. Thérèse suggests that God's word provides the nourishment we need. She agrees that God's word is a lamp for her feet. God's word always provided her with direction in her own spiritual journey.Scripture has always held a central role in the life of the Church. God's word delivers an understanding of what it means to be in discipleship of Jesus Christ. The pulse beat of discipleship is love for God and neighbor. To carry out this twofold commandment requires God's grace and a desire to seek God's will in prayer and discernment. As St. Thérèse wrote, "O my Jesus, I love you. I love the Church, my mother. I recall that the smallest act of pure love is of more value to her [the Church] than all other works together" (*Story of a Soul,* 197).

Lent is a time to focus upon what is truly important and what can be left aside. Let us pray that our lives be conformed more and more to the heart of Jesus Christ and to his mission as priest, prophet and king. He gave his life because of a compassionate love for each one of us.

PRAYER

Loving God, draw us to a love for your Word which truly is a Word of life. May we be faithful to our Lenten observance so that our lives may be more generously dedicated to fulfilling your will for us. We ask this through Christ our Lord. Amen.

Gospel

Jesus said to his disciples:

"When the Son of Man comes in his glory, and all the angels with him, he will sit upon his glorious throne, and all the nations will be assembled before him. And he will separate them one from another, as a shepherd separates the sheep from the goats. He will place the sheep on his right and the goats on his left. Then the king will say to those on his right, 'Come, you who are blessed by my Father. Inherit the kingdom prepared for you from the foundation of the world. For I was hungry and you gave me food, I was thirsty and you gave me drink, a stranger and you welcomed me, naked and you clothed me, ill and you cared for me, in prison and you visited me.' Then the righteous will answer him and say, 'Lord, when did we see you hungry and feed you, or thirsty and give you drink? When did we see you a stranger and welcome you, or naked and clothe you? When did we see you ill or in prison, and visit you?' And the king will say to them in reply, 'Amen, I say to you, whatever you did for one of these least brothers of mine, you did for me.' Then he will say to those on his left, 'Depart from me, you accursed, into the eternal fire prepared for the Devil and his angels. For I was hungry and you gave me no food, I was thirsty and you gave me no drink, a stranger and you gave me no welcome, naked and you gave me no clothing, ill and in prison, and you did not care for me.' Then they will answer and say, 'Lord, when did we see you hungry or thirsty or a stranger or naked or ill or in prison, and not minister to your needs?' He will answer them, 'Amen, I say to you, what you did not do for one of these least ones, you did not do for me.' And these will go off to eternal punishment, but the righteous to eternal life."

Matthew 25: 31-46

ST. THÉRÈSE OF LISIEUX

"Yes, I feel it; even though I had on my conscience all the sins that can be committed, I would go, my heart broken with sorrow, and throw myself into Jesus' arms, for I know how much He loves the prodigal child who returns to Him" (Story of a Soul, 259).

REFLECTION

It is obvious in the Gospel reading from Matthew that Jesus identifies with those who have needs or troubles, namely, the hungry, the thirsty, the prisoner, the sick, those who are naked. In fact the response or nonresponse we give to those who are suffering will determine the outcome of our own lives. The point is that we will be held accountable for our decisions. We cannot simply turn our backs on others. The Gospel scene can disturb our complacency and perhaps move us to recognize our apathy toward the plight of others. We can be open to accept a call to repentance and conversion.

St. Thérèse offers us a message of hope. Our sins should never have the final say about our lives. St. Thérèse tells us that Jesus always accepts the prodigal child. Jesus regards all sinners with merciful love. Conversion is rooted in our desire to relate to Jesus Christ with integrity. We receive pardon and healing for our sins through the sacrament of reconciliation. This sacrament allows us to confess our sins and to do some penance to make up for our sins. The sacrament offers a healthy way to come to terms with the call to conversion. The sacrament fits the Lenten call to become a new creation.

PRAYER

Lord, our God, help each one of us to meet the call to conversion and to new life. Today we offer you our praise and thanksgiving for the wonders of your grace and the beauty of your compassion toward us. We make our prayer through Christ our Lord. Amen.

GOSPEL

JESUS SAID TO HIS DISCIPLES:

"In praying, do not babble like the pagans, who think that they will be heard because of their many words. Do not be like them. Your Father knows what you need before you ask him.

"This is how you are to pray:

Our Father who art in heaven,
hallowed be thy name,
thy Kingdom come,
thy will be done,
on earth as it is in heaven.
Give us this day our daily bread;
and forgive us our trespasses,
as we forgive those who trespass against us;
and lead us not into temptation,
but deliver us from evil.

"If you forgive men their transgressions, your heavenly Father will forgive you. But if you do not forgive men, neither will your Father forgive your transgressions."

MATTHEW 6: 7-15

ST. THÉRÈSE OF LISIEUX

"Sometimes when my mind is in such a great aridity that it is impossible to draw forth one single thought to unite me with God, I very slowly *recite an 'Our Father' and then the angelic salutation; then these Prayers give me great delight; they nourish my soul much more than if I had recited them precipitately a hundred times" (Story of a Soul,* 243).

REFLECTION

The most fundamental expression of our relationship to God is in prayer. Jesus taught his disciples the "Our Father," which expresses a dependence on God's intercession. Jesus asks them not to babble on with many words. Such prayer is not necessary nor does the length of one's prayer effect the outcome. Jesus simply wants our hearts and our trust in Him.

St. Thérèse found the Our Father to be a source of strength when she experienced aridity or dryness in prayer. For St. Thérèse the "Our Father" needs to be prayed slowly, meditatively. In this way we can experience nourishment. In prayer we are mindful of God and we meet the Father who is always mindful of us in His love.

PRAYER

Loving and forgiving God, today we offer you praise. May our prayer be a daily testimony to our love for You. May our lives be faithful in following your Son, Jesus Christ, our Lord. Amen.

GOSPEL

While still more people gathered in the crowd, Jesus said to them, "This generation is an evil generation; it seeks a sign, but no sign will be given it, except the sign of Jonah. Just as Jonah became a sign to the Ninevites, so will the Son of Man be to this generation. At the judgment the queen of the south will rise with the men of this generation and she will condemn them, because she came from the ends of the earth to hear the wisdom of Solomon, and there is something greater than Solomon here. At the judgment the men of Nineveh will arise with this generation and condemn it, because at the preaching of Jonah they repented, and there is something greater than Jonah here."

LUKE 11: 29-32

ST. THÉRÈSE OF LISIEUX

"You know, Mother, I have always wanted to be a saint. Alas! I have always noticed that when I compared myself to the saints, there is between them and me the same difference that exists between a mountain whose summit is lost in the clouds and the obscure grain of sand trampled underfoot by passers-by. Instead of becoming discouraged, I said to myself: God cannot inspire unrealistic desires. I can, then, in spite of my littleness, aspire to holiness" (Story of a Soul, 207).

REFLECTION

The story in Luke reveals a people who resist God's word and refuse to obey the Lord. As a consequence they are viewed as an "evil generation." Lent is a time in which we are invited again to open our minds and hearts to Christian discipleship. Why should we be so resistant to God's word? After all, we are part of a love story and our response to God's invitation is essential to the narrative.

St. Thérèse gave her heart to the Lord. She wanted to become a saint. Yet she believed that while she had no strength of gifts, she still desired intimacy with God. She accepted the fact that God plants the seed of desire for Him in us and we are restless until we decide to love Him with all of our heart.

PRAYER

Lord of all life, during the Lenten season we try to awaken our hearts to your love for us. Our way to you involves the gifts of faith, hope and love. Increase them in us so that we can set aside all other desires and so center our lives in you. We make our prayer through Christ our Lord. Amen.

GOSPEL

JESUS SAID TO HIS DISCIPLES:

"Ask and it will be given to you; seek and you will find; knock and the door will be opened to you. For everyone who asks, receives; and the one who seeks, finds; and to the one who knocks, the door will be opened. Which one of you would hand his son a stone when he asked for a loaf of bread, or a snake when he asked for a fish? If you then, who are wicked, know how to give good gifts to your children, how much more will your heavenly Father give good things to those who ask him.

"Do to others whatever you would have them do to you. This is the law and the prophets."

MATTHEW 7: 7-12

ST. THÉRÈSE OF LISIEUX

"Ah! Lord, I know you don't command the impossible. You know better than I do my weakness and imperfection; You know very well that never would I be able to love my Sisters as You love them, unless You, O my Jesus, loved them in me. It is because You wanted to give me this grace that You made Your new commandment. Oh! How I love this new commandment since it gives me the assurance that Your Will is to love in me all those You command me to love" (Story of a Soul, 221).

REFLECTION

Jesus challenges us to do to others whatever we would have them do to us. This invitation might appear to be an overwhelming task. We meet people who are difficult, cranky, mean, adversarial. Yet, we decide the kind of person we will become. We need to make up our minds about manifesting God's love.

St. Thérèse provides a view in which God is with us and gives us the grace to love with His own love. This she calls the beauty of the new commandment.

PRAYER

Lord, we want to be open to your presence in us. Help us to reach out with gracious hospitality to those who seek our assistance. Becoming holy is your work of grace in us. May we have the strength to accept that grace which can bring about new life. We make our prayer through Christ our Lord. Amen.

GOSPEL

JESUS SAID TO HIS DISCIPLES:

"I tell you, unless your righteousness surpasses that of the scribes and Pharisees, you will not enter into the Kingdom of heaven.

"You have heard that it was said to your ancestors, *You shall not kill; and whoever kills will be liable to judgment.* But I say to you, whoever is angry with his brother will be liable to judgment, and whoever says to his brother, *Raqa,* will be answerable to the Sanhedrin, and whoever says, 'You fool,' will be liable to fiery Gehenna. Therefore, if you bring your gift to the altar, and there recall that your brother has anything against you, leave your gift there at the altar, go first and be reconciled with your brother, and then come and offer your gift. Settle with your opponent quickly while on the way to court. Otherwise your opponent will hand you over to the judge, and the judge will hand you over to the guard, and you will be thrown into prison. Amen, I say to you, you will not be released until you have paid the last penny."

MATTHEW 5: 20-26

ST. THÉRÈSE OF LISIEUX

"There is in the Community a Sister who has the faculty of displeasing me in everything, in her ways, her words, her character, everything seems very disagreeable to me. And still, she is a holy religious who must be very pleasing to God. Not wishing to give in to the natural antipathy I was experiencing, I told

myself that charity must not consist in feelings but in works; then I set myself to doing for this Sister what I would do for the person I loved the most. Each time I met her I prayed to God for her, offering Him all her virtues and merits. I felt this was pleasing to Jesus, for there is no artist who doesn't love to receive praise for his works, and Jesus, the Artist of souls, is happy when we don't stop at the exterior, but penetrating into the inner sanctuary where He chooses to dwell, we admire its beauty" (Story of a Soul, 222).

REFLECTION

The call of today's Gospel is to seek reconciliation wherever there is dissension or animosity or anger. The call of the Lenten season is to be open to change and to a pattern of virtuous living. The work of the Holy Spirit will urge us to recognize and to respond to the call of grace.

St. Thérèse of Lisieux presents us with a person she cannot seem to tolerate. Everything about the woman, a Sister in her Community, she finds "very disagreeable." What can St. Thérèse or even any one of us do in such circumstances? Simply put: it is necessary to fight feelings and to provide "our enemy" with little gestures of love or charity. After all, every human being comes from the hand of the Divine artist and thus is worthy of our respect.

PRAYER

Lord, in our relationships to people there are some who try very much our patience and our good will. We are tempted to recoil and to seek a comfortable distance from them. In this Lenten season give us the courage to accept the cross and to foster relationships that reveal the work of reconciliation and peace. We make our prayer through Christ our Lord. Amen.

GOSPEL

JESUS SAID TO HIS DISCIPLES:

"You have heard that it was said, *You shall love your neighbor and hate your enemy.* But I say to you, love your enemies, and pray for those who persecute you, that you may be children of your heavenly Father, for he makes his sun rise on the bad and the good, and causes rain to fall on the just and the unjust. For if you love those who love you, what recompense will you have? Do not the tax collectors do the same? And if you greet your brothers and sisters only, what is unusual about that? Do not the pagans do the same? So be perfect, just as your heavenly Father is perfect."

MATTHEW 5: 43-48

ST. THÉRÈSE OF LISIEUX

"No doubt, we don't have any enemies in Carmel but there are feelings. One feels attracted to this Sister, whereas with regard to another, one would make a long detour to avoid meeting her. And so, without even knowing it, she becomes the subject of persecution. Well, Jesus is telling me that it is this Sister who must be loved, she must be prayed for even though her conduct would lead me to believe that she doesn't love me" (Story of a Soul, 225).

REFLECTION

The will of God is clear: love your enemies. St. Thérèse reflects in some measure the cost of loving someone we do not like. Obviously, to confront our own antipathy towards a person can produce stress in us. Yet the Lord does not ask the impossible. We can gradually change and God's grace urges us to new life. Again, love is not a matter of feelings but of action on behalf of another.

St. Thérèse has made the point that perhaps we can only offer modest gestures of charity: an affirming word, a smile, a simple service. But our action is done out of genuine love, supernatural love. God's grace enables us to overcome our stubbornness and ill will.

PRAYER

Let us pray.

Gracious and loving God, help us to overcome any resentment or negative attitude which we may maintain towards another. Help us to develop generous and compassionate hearts in the service of all. We make our prayer through Christ, our Lord. Amen.

SECOND WEEK
OF
LENT

GOSPEL

Jesus took Peter, James, and John his brother, and led them up a high mountain by themselves. And he was transfigured before them; his face shone like the sun and his clothes became white as light. And behold, Moses and Elijah appeared to them, conversing with him. Then Peter said to Jesus in reply, "Lord, it is good that we are here. If you wish, I will make three tents here, one for you, one for Moses, and one for Elijah." While he was still speaking, behold, a bright cloud cast a shadow over them, then from the cloud came a voice that said, "This is my beloved Son, with whom I am well pleased; listen to him." When the disciples heard this, they fell prostrate and were very much afraid. But Jesus came and touched them, saying, "Rise, and do not be afraid." And when the disciples raised their eyes, they saw no one else but Jesus alone.

As they were coming down from the mountain, Jesus charged them, "Do not tell the vision to anyone until the Son of Man has been raised from the dead."

MATTHEW 17: 1-9

ST. THÉRÈSE OF LISIEUX

"My God, I already hear your eternal feast being prepared . . . . After this life's exile I'll go to see my Father's house again" ("The Canticle of Celine," in *The Poetry of St. Thérèse*, 102).

REFLECTION

"Listen to Him" is the voice heard during the Transfiguration. And how do we listen to God? By attending to God's word in Scripture, by the voice of tradition, by discerning God's presence in the events of our lives and our history.

St. Thérèse can hear the eternal banquet being prepared because her heart is totally centered in the will of God. Our Lenten penance should help us to develop an ear for God's word being communicated in our prayer, our relationships, our work. Listen to Him.

PRAYER

O Lord, teach me the wisdom I need to recognize your presence in my life. May I always listen to your word, to your teaching, to your challenges, and follow you faithfully. We make our prayer through Christ our Lord. Amen.

GOSPEL

Jesus took Peter, James and John and led them up a high mountain apart by themselves. And he was transfigured before them, and his clothes became dazzling white, such as no fuller on earth could bleach them. Then Elijah appeared to them along with Moses, and they were conversing with Jesus. Then Peter said to Jesus in reply, "Rabbi, it is good that we are here! Let us make three tents: one for you, one for Moses, and one for Elijah." He hardly knew what to say, they were so terrified. Then a cloud came, casting a shadow over them; from the cloud came a voice, "This is my beloved Son. Listen to him." Suddenly, looking around, they no longer saw anyone but Jesus alone with them.

As they were coming down from the mountain, he charged them not to relate what they had seen to anyone, except when the Son of Man had risen from the dead. So they kept the matter to themselves, questioning what rising from the dead meant.

MARK 9: 2-10

ST. THÉRÈSE OF LISIEUX

"Yes, I feel it, when I am charitable, it is Jesus alone who is acting in me, and the more I am united to Him, the more also do I love my Sisters" (Story of a Soul, 221).

REFLECTION

Just as Jesus appeared to be along at the end of the Transfiguration scene, so St. Thérèse believed it was Jesus alone who enabled her to be charitable in her relationship to the Sisters. The more she was united to Jesus the more she was able to love.

In faith we believe that Jesus is at work in each one of us. Lent reminds us that the work of Jesus Christ and the Holy Spirit is to bring about spiritual and human maturity in us. Can we become more patient, more compassionate, more generous in our daily lives? The work of grace is to bring about in us the heart of Jesus Christ.

PRAYER

Lord, our God, help me to see the presence of Christ in my life. May I share the enthusiasm of Peter, James, and John and follow you even if I must bear the Cross. I make this prayer through Christ our Lord. Amen.

GOSPEL

Jesus took Peter, John, and James and went up the mountain to pray. While he was praying his face changed in appearance and his clothing became dazzling white. And behold, two men were conversing with him, Moses and Elijah, who appeared in glory and spoke of his exodus that he was going to accomplish in Jerusalem. Peter and his companions had been overcome by sleep, but becoming fully awake, they saw his glory and the two men standing with him. As they were about to part from him, Peter said to Jesus, "Master, it is good that we are here; let us make three tents, one for you, one for Moses, and one for Elijah." But he did not know what he was saying. While he was still speaking, a cloud came and cast a shadow over them, and they became frightened when they entered the cloud. Then from the cloud came a voice that said, "This is my chosen Son; listen to him." After the voice had spoken, Jesus was found alone. They fell silent and did not at that time tell anyone what they had seen.

LUKE 9: 28B-36

ST. THÉRÈSE OF LISIEUX

"I don't want to be a saint *by halves, I'm not afraid to suffer for You, I fear only one thing: to keep my own will; so take it, for* 'I choose all' *that You will"* (Story of a Soul, 27).

REFLECTION

Jesus was "the chosen Son" of the Father. He was sent by the Father to manifest God's love for us. The mission cost Him his very life. In following Jesus' life and in many cases the lives of his heroic followers, the Saints, we see how cruel and evil, how indifferent and uncaring our world can be.

And so St. Thérèse announces that she does not wish to be a half-hearted saint. Rather she wants to give herself totally to Jesus Christ and to follow God's will no matter what the cost. We need to pray to God to develop the confidence and openness that is characteristic of the saints.

PRAYER

God of all consolation, send your grace to enable us to offer you our total self during this Lenten journey. Help us to let go of those attachments which hold us back from being a total self-gift to you. We make this prayer through Christ our Lord. Amen.

GOSPEL

JESUS SAID TO HIS DISCIPLES:

"Be merciful, just as your Father is merciful.

"Stop judging and you will not be judged. Stop condemning and you will not be condemned. Forgive and you will be forgiven. Give and gifts will be given to you; a good measure, packed together, shaken down, and overflowing, will be poured into your lap. For the measure with which you measure will in return be measured out to you."

LUKE 6: 36-38

ST. THÉRÈSE OF LISIEUX

"I do not hold in contempt beautiful thoughts which nourish the soul and unite it with God; but for a long time I have understood that we must not depend on them and even make perfection consist in receiving many spiritual lights. The most beautiful thoughts are nothing without good works" (Story of a Soul, 234).

REFLECTION

What unites this passage from Luke's Gospel and the quotation from St. Thérèse involves charity. We are called to live a life that manifests mercy and forgiveness for God is merciful.

St. Thérèse recognizes that when spiritual insights come to our mind and heart, we receive consolation and peace. But like St. Teresa before her, St. Thérèse believes that an authentic spiritual life shows itself in good works. We are challenged today to live out our faith in relationships that serve the good of others.

PRAYER

Gracious and merciful God, deepen my desire to serve you all the days of my life. May I bring God's love into the life of others by my compassion, forgiveness, understanding, and service. Your word, O Lord, will bring about new life in me as I continue the Lenten journey. I make this prayer through Christ our Lord. Amen.

GOSPEL

Jesus spoke to the crowds and to his disciples, saying, "The scribes and the Pharisees have taken their seat on the chair of Moses. Therefore, do and observe all things whatsoever they tell you, but do not follow their example. For they preach but they do not practice. They tie up heavy burdens hard to carry and lay them on people's shoulders, but they will not lift a finger to move them. All their works are performed to be seen. They widen their phylacteries and lengthen their tassels. They love places of honor at banquets, seats of honor in synagogues, greetings in marketplaces, and the salutation 'Rabbi.' As for you, do not be called 'Rabbi.' You have but one teacher, and you are all brothers. Call no one on earth your father; you have but one Father in heaven. Do not be called 'Master'; you have but one master, the Christ. The greatest among you must be your servant. Whoever exalts himself will be humbled; but whoever humbles himself will be exalted."

MATTHEW 23: 1-12

ST. THÉRÈSE OF LISIEUX

"My dear Mother, you can see that I am a very little soul *and that I can offer God only* very little things. *It often happens that I allow these little sacrifices which give such peace to the soul to slip by; this does not discourage me, for I put up with having a little less peace and I try to be more vigilant on another occasion"* *(Story of a Soul, 250).*

REFLECTION

The contrast between the behavior of the scribes and Pharisees and the humble posture of St. Thérèse reveals the secret of the Gospel. We are not called to lord it over others or to be noticed as important or to be held in fear by others. Rather, we are called to be brothers and sisters to one another insofar as we can be of service to each other.

Our service of others may like St. Thérèse be made up of "little sacrifices" such as assisting the elderly in shopping or bringing a meal to a shut-in. It may mean listening to someone's painful story of rejection or hurt. Or perhaps we remain silent when criticized by another. Concern for the welfare of others who struggle is evident in the lives of the humble.

PRAYER

Father of our Lord Jesus Christ, stir up our hearts so that we may be sensitive to the struggles of others. May we have the wisdom to know how to respond to our brothers and sisters, so that the presence of God is revealed in our lives. We ask this through Christ our Lord. Amen.

GOSPEL

As Jesus was going up to Jerusalem, he took the Twelve disciples aside by themselves, and said to them on the way, "Behold, we are going up to Jerusalem, and the Son of Man will be handed over to the chief priests and the scribes, and they will condemn him to death, and hand him over to the Gentiles to be mocked and scourged and crucified, and he will be raised on the third day."

Then the mother of the sons of Zebedee approached Jesus with her sons and did him homage, wishing to ask him for something. He said to her, "What do you wish?" She answered him, "Command that these two sons of mine sit, one at your right and the other at your left, in your kingdom." Jesus said in reply, "You do not know what you are asking. Can you drink the chalice that I am going to drink?" They said to him, "We can." He replied, "My chalice you will indeed drink, but to sit at my right and at my left, this is not mine to give but is for those for whom it has been prepared by my Father." When the ten heard this, they became indignant at the two brothers. But Jesus summoned them and said, "You know that the rulers of the Gentiles lord it over them, and the great ones make their authority over them felt. But it shall not be so among you. Rather, whoever wishes to be great among you shall be your servant; whoever wishes to be first among you shall be your slave. Just so, the Son of Man did not come to be served but to serve and to give his life as a ransom for many."

MATTHEW 20: 17-28

ST. THÉRÈSE OF LISIEUX

"How did Jesus love His disciples and why did He love them? Ah! It was not their natural qualities that could have attracted Him, since there was between Him and them an infinite distance. He was knowledge, Eternal Wisdom, while they were poor ignorant fishermen filled with earthly thoughts. And still Jesus called them friends, His brothers. *He desires to see them reign with Him in the kingdom of His Father, and to open that kingdom to them He wills to die on the cross, for He said:* 'Greater love than this no man has than that he lay down his life for his friends' *(Story of a Soul, 220).*

REFLECTION

The image of relationship is reflected throughout the pages of Scripture. Today's Gospel calls us to relationships which show respect and esteem for each other. Jesus manifested an unsurpassable love for us by giving his life for us. He was "mocked and scourged and crucified" but through his death we were given new life, the forgiveness of our sins, and the promise of eternal life with him.

St. Thérèse notes how Jesus related to his disciples. She saw no special reason why Jesus, the eternal Son of God, should be attracted to them. Yet he treated them as brothers. We walk in the footsteps of Christ when we provide an open and affirming style of relationship. Not all relationships are easy. Some are challenging, others are hurtful. When we carry an open attitude we allow for the possibility of reconciliation and peace.

PRAYER

Let us pray.

Gracious and loving Father, you tell us to live as servants of one another. May we embrace the virtue of humility so as to serve you, O Lord, present within the hearts of all people. Thus, our lives can give glory to You, O Lord. We make our prayer through Christ our Lord. Amen.

GOSPEL

JESUS SAID TO THE PHARISEES:

"There was a rich man who dressed in purple garments and fine linen and dined sumptuously each day. And lying at his door was a poor man named Lazarus, covered with sores, who would gladly have eaten his fill of the scraps that fell from the rich man's table. Dogs even used to come and lick his sores. When the poor man died, he was carried away by angels to the bosom of Abraham. The rich man also died and was buried, and from the netherworld, where he was in torment, he raised his eyes and saw Abraham far off and Lazarus at his side. And he cried out, 'Father Abraham, have pity on me. Send Lazarus to dip the tip of his finger in water and cool my tongue, for I am suffering torment in these flames.' Abraham replied, 'My child, remember that you received what was good during your lifetime while Lazarus likewise received what was bad; but now he is comforted here, whereas you are tormented. Moreover, between us and you a great chasm is established to prevent anyone from crossing who might wish to go from our side to yours or from your side to ours.' He said, 'Then I beg you, father, send him to my father's house, for I have five brothers, so that he may warn them, lest they too come to this place of torment.' But Abraham replied, 'They have Moses and the prophets. Let them listen to them.' He said, 'Oh no, father Abraham, but if someone from the dead goes to them, they will repent.' Then Abraham said, 'If they will not listen to Moses and the prophets, neither will they be persuaded if someone should rise from the dead.'"

LUKE 16: 19-31

ST. THÉRÈSE OF LISIEUX

"Dear Mother, this is my Prayer. I ask Jesus to draw me into the flames of His love, to unite me so closely to Him that He live and act in me. I feel that the more the fire of love burns within my heart, the more I shall say 'Draw me,' *the more also the souls who will approach me (poor little piece of iron, useless if I withdraw from the divine furnace), the more these souls* will run swiftly in the odor of the ointments of their Beloved, *for a soul that is burning with love cannot remain inactive"* (Story of a Soul, 257).

REFLECTION

The rich man in the Gospel story thought that he had offered a reasonable request. Since he had failed to care for Lazarus at his doorstep and ended in torment, what if a messenger would warn his five brothers so that they would not make the same mistake? The answer is that the rich man's brothers have Moses and the prophets. Let them listen to the prophets and awaken to God's call. God speaks through his prophets.

St. Thérèse helps us to see that it is in uniting with Jesus in love that we encounter the will of God. It is God's love which enables us to see how we are to respond in life. St. Thérèse's point is that when we burn with love we cannot remain inactive. In other words, love moves us to become acclimated to God's love for others. As a result we could never ignore Lazarus at our doorstep.

PRAYER

Father in heaven, hear our prayer and guide us toward holiness of life. May we be able to help those in need, especially those who are poor like Lazarus. Enable us to be your prophets in a world which needs to discover the presence of God. We ask this through Christ our Lord. Amen.

GOSPEL

JESUS SAID TO THE CHIEF PRIESTS AND
THE ELDERS OF THE PEOPLE:

"Hear another parable. There was a landowner who planted a vineyard, put a hedge around it, dug a wine press in it, and built a tower. Then he leased it to tenants and went on a journey. When vintage time drew near, he sent his servants to the tenants to obtain his produce. But the tenants seized the servants and one they beat, another they killed, and a third they stoned. Again he sent other servants, more numerous than the first ones, but they treated them in the same way. Finally, he sent his son to them, thinking, 'They will respect my son.' But when the tenants saw the son, they said to one another, 'This is the heir. Come, let us kill him and acquire his inheritance.' They seized him, threw him out of the vineyard, and killed him. What will the owner of the vineyard do to those tenants when he comes?" They answered him, "He will put those wretched men to a wretched death and lease his vineyard to other tenants who will give him the produce at the proper times." Jesus said to them, "Did you never read in the Scriptures:

The stone that the builders rejected
has become the cornerstone;
by the Lord has this been done,
and it is wonderful in our eyes?

Therefore, I say to you, the Kingdom of God will be taken away from you and given to a people that will produce its fruit."

When the chief priests and the Pharisees heard his parables, they knew that he was speaking about them. And although they were attempting to arrest him, they feared the crowds, for they regarded him as a prophet.

MATTHEW 21: 33-43, 45-46

ST. THÉRÈSE OF LISIEUX

"I know that Jesus cannot desire useless sufferings for me, and that he would not inspire the longings I feel unless he wanted to grant them.

Oh! How sweet the way of love! How I want to apply myself to doing the will of God always with the greatest self-surrender!" (Story of a Soul, 181).

REFLECTION

The reading from the Gospel of St. Matthew contrasts with the reading from St. Thérèse. The Gospel story tells of tenants who will do violence to achieve their goal: to acquire the owner's inheritance. Their behavior only aroused the owner's sense of justice. The owner's property will be put into the hands of new tenants.

St. Thérèse centers her life in doing God's will. Her theocentric ways moved her to self-surrender to Jesus even in the midst of suffering, because with Jesus there is no useless suffering. What makes all possible is commitment to God's love in Christ Jesus. Suffering given to the Lord helps to bring about a new creation.

PRAYER

Lord, help me to center my heart in following Jesus Christ. Enable me to overcome the selfish motives in my life that dominated the behavior of the tenants. Like St. Thérèse, may I surrender my life to you who are Lord of all creation. We make our prayer through Christ our Lord. Amen.

GOSPEL

Tax collectors and sinners were all drawing near to listen to Jesus, but the Pharisees and scribes began to complain, saying, "This man welcomes sinners and eats with them." So to them Jesus addressed this parable. "A man had two sons, and the younger son said to his father, 'Father, give me the share of your estate that should come to me.' So the father divided the property between them. After a few days, the younger son collected all his belongings and set off to a distant country where he squandered his inheritance on a life of dissipation. When he had freely spent everything, a severe famine struck that country, and he found himself in dire need. So he hired himself out to one of the local citizens who sent him to his farm to tend the swine. And he longed to eat his fill of the pods on which the swine fed, but nobody gave him any. Coming to his senses he thought, 'How many of my father's hired workers have more than enough food to eat, but here am I, dying from hunger. I shall get up and go to my father and I shall say to him, "Father, I have sinned against heaven and against you. I no longer deserve to be called your son; treat me as you would treat one of your hired workers."' So he got up and went back to his father. While he was still a long way off, his father caught sight of him, and was filled with compassion. He ran to his son, embraced him and kissed him. His son said to him, 'Father, I have sinned against heaven and against you; I no longer deserve to be called your son.' But his father ordered his servants, 'Quickly, bring the finest robe and put it on him; put a ring on his finger and sandals on his feet. Take the fattened calf and slaughter it. Then let us celebrate with a feast, because this son of mine was dead, and has come to life again; he was lost, and has been found.' Then the celebration began. Now the older son had been out in the field and, on his way back, as he neared the house, he heard the sound of music and dancing. He called one of the servants and asked what this might mean. The servant said to him, 'Your brother has returned and your father has slaughtered the fattened calf because he has him back safe and sound.' He became angry, and when he refused to enter the house, his father came out and pleaded with him. He said to his father in reply, 'Look, all these years I served you and not once did I disobey your orders; yet you never gave me even a young goat to feast on with my friends. But when your son returns who swallowed up your property with prostitutes, for him you slaughter the fattened calf.' He said to him, 'My son, you are here with me always; everything I have is yours. But now we must celebrate and rejoice, because your brother was dead and has come to life again; he was lost and has been found.'"

LUKE 15: 1-3, 11-32

ST. THÉRÈSE OF LISIEUX

"I was at the most dangerous age for young girls, but God did for me what Ezechiel reports in his prophecies: 'Passing by me, Jesus saw that the time had come for me to be loved. He entered into a covenant with me and I became His *own. He spread his mantle over me, he washed me with precious perfumes. He reclothed me in embroidered robes, He gave me priceless necklaces and ornaments. He nourished me with purest flour, with honey and oil in* abundance. *Then I became beautiful in His eyes an He made me a mighty queen'" (Story of a Soul, 101–2; see also Ez 16:8–13).*

REFLECTION

Recognizing God's saving grace in life brings about celebration and gestures of love. The well known Gospel reading from St. Luke, the story of the Prodigal Son, reveals a conversion account in which a wayward son turns away from a sinful life. The Father says to the older son: "your brother was dead and has come to life again, he was lost and has been found." The father in the story portrays God's mercy and forgiveness.

St. Thérèse's comment reveals God's love for her before anything untoward or sinful could erupt in her life. Jesus established a covenant with St. Thérèse and she became beautiful to the Lord. The oil she received in abundance was the inspiration she derived from the Imitation of Christ and particularly from the four Gospels. Implied in her reflection is the value of spiritual reading for a holy life. God brings life to us in the ordinary and the routine. Very often God's grace enables us to turn away from temptation and the attraction of sin.

PRAYER

Loving God, enable each one of us to open our hearts to you. Teach us the ways of fidelity and true love for you and for our neighbor. We make our prayer through Christ our Lord. Amen.

THIRD WEEK
OF
LENT

GOSPEL

Jesus came to a town of Samaria called Sychar, near the plot of land that Jacob had given to his son Joseph. Jacob's well was there. Jesus, tired from his journey, sat down there at the well. It was about noon.

A woman of Samaria came to draw water. Jesus said to her, "Give me a drink." His disciples had gone into the town to buy food. The Samaritan woman said to him, "How can you, a Jew, ask me, a Samaritan woman, for a drink?" — For Jews use nothing in common with Samaritans. — Jesus answered and said to her, "If you knew the gift of God and who is saying to you, 'Give me a drink,' you would have asked him and he would have given you living water." The woman said to him, "Sir, you do not even have a bucket and the cistern is deep; where then can you get this living water? Are you greater than our father Jacob, who gave us this cistern and drank from it himself with his children and his flocks?" Jesus answered and said to her, "Everyone who drinks this water will be thirsty again; but whoever drinks the water I shall give will never thirst; the water I shall give will become in him a spring of water welling up to eternal life." The woman said to him, "Sir, give me this water, so that I may not be thirsty or have to keep coming here to draw water."

Jesus said to her, "Go call your husband and come back." The woman answered and said to him, "I do not have a husband." Jesus answered her, "You are right in saying, 'I do not have a husband.' For you have had five husbands, and the one you have now is not your husband. What you have said is true." The woman said to him, "Sir, I can see that you are a prophet. Our ancestors worshiped on this mountain; but you people say that the place to worship is in Jerusalem." Jesus said to her, "Believe me, woman, the hour is coming when you will worship the Father neither on this mountain nor in Jerusalem. You people worship what you do not understand; we worship what we understand, because salvation is from the Jews. But the hour is coming, and is now here, when true worshipers will worship the Father in Spirit and truth; and indeed the

Father seeks such people to worship him. God is Spirit, and those who worship him must worship in Spirit and truth." The woman said to him, "I know that the Messiah is coming, the one called the Christ; when he comes, he will tell us everything." Jesus said to her, "I am he, the one speaking with you."

At that moment his disciples returned, and were amazed that he was talking with a woman, but still no one said, "What are you looking for?" or "Why are you talking with her?" The woman left her water jar and went into the town and said to the people, "Come see a man who told me everything I have done. Could he possibly be the Christ?" They went out of the town and came to him. Meanwhile, the disciples urged him, "Rabbi, eat." But he said to them, "I have food to eat of which you do not know." So the disciples said to one another, "Could someone have brought him something to eat?" Jesus said to them, "My food is to do the will of the one who sent me and to finish his work. Do you not say, 'In four months the harvest will be here'? I tell you, look up and see the fields ripe for the harvest. The reaper is already receiving payment and gathering crops for eternal life, so that the sower and reaper can rejoice together. For here the saying is verified that 'One sows and another reaps.' I sent you to reap what you have not worked for; others have done the work, and you are sharing the fruits of their work."

Many of the Samaritans of that town began to believe in him because of the word of the woman who testified, "He told me everything I have done." When the Samaritans came to him, they invited him to stay with them; and he stayed there two days. Many more began to believe in him because of his word, and they said to the woman, "We no longer believe because of your word; for we have heard for ourselves, and we know that this is truly the savior of the world."

JOHN 4: 5-42

Shorter form: JOHN 4:5-15, 19b-26, 39a, 40-42
Longer form may be optionally read on any day in the third week of Lent

ST. THÉRÈSE OF LISIEUX

"See, then, all that Jesus lays claim to from us; He has no need of our works but only of our love, *for the same God who declares He* has no need to tell us when He is hungry *did not fear to beg for a little water from the Samaritan woman. He was thirsty. But when He said:* 'Give me to drink,' *it was the* love *of His poor creature the Creator of the universe was seeking. He was thirsty for love. Ah! I feel it more than ever before, Jesus is* parched, *for He meets only the ungrateful and indifferent among His disciples in the world, and among* His own disciples, *alas, He finds few hearts who surrender to Him without reservations, who understand the real tenderness of His infinite Love" (Story of a Soul,* 189).

REFLECTION

The reading from the Gospel of St. John reveals the encounter between Jesus and the Samaritan woman. The woman is amazed that Jesus knows so much about her. She wonders if He is the Christ. Jesus tells her that relationship to Him will fulfill all thirst and bring about new life. The woman acknowledges that He is the Christ. She tells the townspeople her experience and many are drawn to Jesus. The search for the Messiah is over.

St. Thérèse adds that Jesus was looking for the Samaritan woman to find her fulfillment in Him. Only Jesus can satisfy our longing for meaning. St. Thérèse sees that Jesus seeks our love. Our love needs to come to self-surrender in Him. Jesus' desire for our love is brought out further in one of St. Thérèse's plays: "The Divine Beggar at Christmas." The image is provocative: Jesus is begging for our love and our friendship. Conversion begins by naming our longing: our desire in depth is to love our Lord.

PRAYER

Gracious God, help us to realize that our deepest desire is to love you and to live your Gospel. May we be able to overcome any indifference in our heart so that our fulfillment can come about in our relationship to you. We ask this through Christ our Lord. Amen.

GOSPEL

Since the Passover of the Jews was near, Jesus went up to Jerusalem. He found in the temple area those who had sold oxen, sheep and doves, as well as the money changers seated there. He made a whip out of cords and drove them all out of the temple area, with sheep and oxen, and spilled the coins of the money changers and overturned their tables, and to those who sold doves he said, "Take these out of here, and stop making my Father's house a marketplace." His disciples recalled the words of Scripture, *Zeal for your house will consume me.* At this the Jews answered and said to him, "What sign can you show us for doing this?" Jesus answered and said to them, "Destroy this temple and in three days I will raise it up." The Jews said, "This temple has been under construction for forty-six years, and you will raise it up in three days?" But he was speaking about the temple of his body. Therefore, when he was raised from the dead, his disciples remembered that he had said this, and they came to believe the Scripture and the word Jesus had spoken.

While he was in Jerusalem for the feast of Passover, many began to believe in his name when they saw the signs he was doing. But Jesus would not trust himself to them because he knew them all, and did not need anyone to testify about human nature. He himself understood it well.

JOHN 2: 13-25

ST. THÉRÈSE OF LISIEUX

"It is not to remain in a golden ciborium that He comes to us each day *from heaven; it's to find another heaven, infinitely more dear to Him than the first: the heaven of our soul, made to His image, the living temple of the adorable Trinity!"* (Story of a Soul, 104).

REFLECTION

What unites our two readings today is zeal. Zeal is fervor, eagerness expressed in the pursuit of a goal. Jesus wishes to show His love and his communion with the Father. He wants to affirm the need for respect for the Temple, his Father's house. The commercialism he finds in the Temple area drives Jesus to clear out the money changers. After all, the Temple is a house of prayer.

St. Thérèse is eager to express her zeal for the Eucharist. Growing up in a time when the remnants of Jansenism[1] affected Eucharistic piety, the frequency of receiving communion, St. Thérèse argues that Jesus wants to come to us each day, to the ciborium of our soul where he dwells in the "adorable Trinity."

PRAYER

Let us pray.

Lord, our God, may we always maintain respect and love for your presence in our lives. May we also respect your presence in the lives of others, no matter the challenge that we face. We make our prayer through Christ our Lord. Amen.

---

3. Jansenism is a movement begun by Cornelius Jansen (1585-1638) in France. It was a form of stern asceticism which arose from a very pessimistic view of humanity. While the movement was condemned by the Church, its influence lingered into the twentieth century. The movement opposed frequent communion, for example, because frequent communion encouraged laxity towards confession.

GOSPEL

Some people told Jesus about the Galileans whose blood Pilate had mingled with the blood of their sacrifices. Jesus said to them in reply, "Do you think that because these Galileans suffered in this way they were greater sinners than all other Galileans? By no means! But I tell you, if you do not repent, you will all perish as they did! Or those eighteen people who were killed when the tower at Siloam fell on them – do you think they were more guilty than everyone else who lived in Jerusalem? By no means! But I tell you, if you do not repent, you will all perish as they did!"

And he told them this parable: "There once was a person who had a fig tree planted in his orchard, and when he came in search of fruit on it but found none, he said to the gardener, 'For three years now I have come in search of fruit on this fig tree but have found none. So cut it down. Why should it exhaust the soil?' "He said to him in reply, 'Sir, leave it for this year also, and I shall cultivate the ground around it and fertilize it; it may bear fruit in the future. If not you can cut it down.'"

LUKE 13: 1-9

ST. THÉRÈSE OF LISIEUX

"Yes, I feel it; even though I had on my conscience all the sins that can be committed, I would go, my heart broken with sorrow, and throw myself into Jesus' arms, for I know how much He loves the prodigal child who returns to Him" (Story of a Soul, 259).

REFLECTION

Repentance is a process of turning away from deliberate sin and living with a firm purpose of amendment. This process of conversion is identified as the purgative stage in the spiritual journey. We seek to move into living a virtuous life.

St. Thérèse makes clear that repentance always insures God's merciful love toward us and God's forgiveness of our sins. Notice that St. Thérèse mentions sorrow for sin as a prerequisite for enjoying the Lord's reconciling love.

PRAYER

Loving Father, often we need your forgiveness for our selfish and arrogant ways. Help us to seek you above all and thereby come to know your gracious love for us. We make our prayer through Christ our Lord. Amen.

GOSPEL

JESUS SAID TO THE PEOPLE IN THE SYNAGOGUE
AT NAZARETH:

"Amen, I say to you, no prophet is accepted in his own native place.
Indeed, I tell you, there were many widows in Israel in the days of Elijah
when the sky was closed for three and a half years and a severe famine
spread over the entire land. It was to none of these that Elijah was sent,
but only to a widow in Zarephath in the land of Sidon. Again, there
were many lepers in Israel during the time of Elisha the prophet; yet
not one of them was cleansed, but only Naaman the Syrian." When
the people in the synagogue heard this, they were all filled with fury.
They rose up, drove him out of the town, and led him to the brow of
the hill on which their town had been built, to hurl him down head-
long. But he passed through the midst of them and went away.

LUKE 4: 24-30

ST. THÉRÈSE OF LISIEUX

*"Remembering the Prayer of Elisha to his Father Elijah when he dared
to ask him for HIS DOUBLE SPIRIT, I presented myself before the
angels and saints and I said to them: 'I am the smallest of creatures; I
know my misery and my feebleness, but I know also how much noble and
generous hearts love to do good. I beg you then, O Blessed Inhabitants
of heaven, I beg you to ADOPT ME AS YOUR CHILD. To you alone
will be the glory which you will make me merit, but deign to answer my
Prayer. It is bold, I know; however, I dare to ask you to obtain for me
YOUR TWOFOLD LOVE" (Story of a Soul, 195–96).*

REFLECTION

Both readings speak of Elijah the prophet who was highly regarded by the Israelites. He conquered the false gods of Baal and served God in truth and in justice.

St. Thérèse wants to receive a double portion of his spirit as did the prophet Elisha. For St. Thérèse Elijah represents a prophet with life-giving energy. St. Thérèse seeks a double portion of Elijah's strength so that she can provide a faithful and generous love in community life. In a similar manner each one of us needs this gracious life-giving energy to strengthen our commitments to family life and to our other responsibilities.

PRAYER

Let us pray.

Loving Father, provide us with the gracious spirit of Elijah the prophet so that we may witness to your presence in all circumstances and before all whom we meet. We ask this through Christ our Lord. Amen.

GOSPEL

Peter approached Jesus and asked him, "Lord, if my brother sins against me, how often must I forgive him? As many as seven times?" Jesus answered, "I say to you, not seven times but seventy-seven times. That is why the Kingdom of heaven may be likened to a king who decided to settle accounts with his servants. When he began the accounting, a debtor was brought before him who owed him a huge amount. Since he had no way of paying it back, his master ordered him to be sold, along with his wife, his children, and all his property, in payment of the debt. At that, the servant fell down, did him homage, and said, 'Be patient with me, and I will pay you back in full.' Moved with compassion the master of that servant let him go and forgave him the loan. When that servant had left, he found one of his fellow servants who owed him a much smaller amount. He seized him and started to choke him, demanding, 'Pay back what you owe.' Falling to his knees, his fellow servant begged him, 'Be patient with me, and I will pay you back.' But he refused. Instead, he had him put in prison until he paid back the debt. Now when his fellow servants saw what had happened, they were deeply disturbed, and went to their master and reported the whole affair. His master summoned him and said to him, 'You wicked servant! I forgave you your entire debt because you begged me to. Should you not have had pity on your fellow servant, as I had pity on you?' Then in anger his master handed him over to the torturers until he should pay back the whole debt. So will my heavenly Father do to you, unless each of you forgives your brother from your heart."

MATTHEW 18: 21-35

ST. THÉRÈSE OF LISIEUX

"As a father has tenderness for his children, so the Lord has compassion on us" (St. Thérèse's letter to Pere Roulland, letter 226, 1093).[1]

REFLECTION

It can be very difficult for us to forgive someone who has hurt us by word or action. All of us are fragile human beings. Yet, we need to be mindful that we have been forgiven by God even though we have abused His law and manipulated His people. Like St. Thérèse we need to acknowledge the tenderness of God. We can let go of hurts and bring mercy and forgiveness to others. In doing so we are disciples of the Son of God. Why should we carry grudges and antagonisms within? Neither provides us with peace and tranquility, both signs of God's presence within.

PRAYER

Let us pray.

Father in heaven, enable me to let go of past hurts and to cultivate a new heart that is humble and forgiving. I make this prayer through Christ our Lord. Amen.

---

4. *The Letters of St. Thérèse of Lisieux and Those Who Knew Her: General Correspondence (1890–1897),* vol. 2, trans. from the critical edition by John Clarke, O.C.D. (Washington, DC: ICS Publications, 1988). Hereafter, *The Letters of St. Thérèse.*

GOSPEL

JESUS SAID TO HIS DISCIPLES:

"Do not think that I have come to abolish the law or the prophets. I have come not to abolish but to fulfill. Amen, I say to you, until heaven and earth pass away, not the smallest letter or the smallest part of a letter will pass from the law, until all things have taken place. Therefore, whoever breaks one of the least of these commandments and teaches others to do so will be called least in the Kingdom of heaven. But whoever obeys and teaches these commandments will be called greatest in the Kingdom of heaven."

MATTHEW 5: 17-19

ST. THÉRÈSE OF LISIEUX

"Oh! What peace floods the soul when she rises above natural feelings. No, there is no joy comparable to that which the truly poor in spirit experience" (Story of a Soul, 226).

REFLECTION

The poor in spirit recognize that everything good in life comes as a gift. The law of God is not perceived as a burden but rather as a way to grow in Christian discipleship. The commandments are given to us so that we can live together in maturity and peace. We need to be mindful that God abides in us and through His Spirit we are moved by grace toward holiness of life.

Mindfulness of God is maintained through the practice of the presence of God, through recollection and through the regular practice of prayer. We grow in our faith in God's love through our recollected heart which is nourished by our love for God's word in Scripture. We grow more able to discern and follow the Spirit of God in our everyday lives. Our lives reflect more and more the peace and joy of living in the presence of God.

PRAYER

God, give me the joy of knowing and following your law. May I discern your will for me to walk in newness of life. We make our prayer through Christ our Lord. Amen.

GOSPEL

Jesus was driving out a demon that was mute, and when the demon had gone out, the mute man spoke and the crowds were amazed. Some of them said, "By the power of Beelzebul, the prince of demons, he drives out demons." Others, to test him, asked him for a sign from heaven. But he knew their thoughts and said to them, "Every kingdom divided against itself will be laid waste and house will fall against house. And if Satan is divided against himself, how will his kingdom stand? For you say that it is by Beelzebul that I drive out demons. If I, then, drive out demons by Beelzebul, by whom do your own people drive them out? Therefore they will be your judges. But if it is by the finger of God that I drive out demons, then the Kingdom of God has come upon you. When a strong man fully armed guards his palace, his possessions are safe. But when one stronger than he attacks and overcomes him, he takes away the armor on which he relied and distributes the spoils. Whoever is not with me is against me, and whoever does not gather with me scatters."

LUKE 11: 14-23

ST. THÉRÈSE OF LISIEUX

"The beautiful day of my wedding finally arrived. It was without a single cloud; however, the preceding evening a storm arose within my soul the like of which I'd never seen before. Not a single doubt concerning my vocation had ever entered my mind until then and it evidently was necessary that I experience this trial. In the evening while making the Way of the Cross after Matins, my vocation appeared to me as a dream, a chimera. I found life in Carmel to be very beautiful, but the devil inspired me with the assurance that it wasn't for me" (Story of a Soul, 166).

REFLECTION

The character of Satan in Scripture portrays one who causes division and doubt, fear and suspicion. In St. Luke's Gospel Jesus has to defend the power He has to overcome evil. Everything he said and did advanced the Kingdom of God. The Kingdom of God includes the call to charity and justice, to grace and new life.

St. Thérèse had her own struggle with the demon before her profession of vows. She did not believe she was worthy of the call. She consulted both her novice mistress and the Prioress of the community. Both assured her that she did have a vocation to Carmel. As soon as she heard the words of affirmation the darkness left her and she was filled with a sense of peace.

The evil one seeks to discourage people, to make them unsure of their worthiness before God. Yet the word of God always serves life and virtue, generosity and love. Faith enables us to cherish God's word and the work of the Holy Spirit within us.

PRAYER

Let us pray.

Lord, our God, help us to resist the attraction of evil and sin in our lives. Keep us centered on your presence in our lives. We make our prayer through Christ our Lord. Amen.

GOSPEL

One of the scribes came to Jesus and asked him, "Which is the first of all the commandments?" Jesus replied, "The first is this: *Hear, O Israel! The Lord our God is Lord alone! You shall love the Lord your God with all your heart, with all your soul, with all your mind, and with all your strength.* The second is this: *You shall love your neighbor as yourself.* There is no other commandment greater than these." The scribe said to him, "Well said, teacher. You are right in saying, *He is One and there is no other than he.* And *to love him with all your heart, with all your understanding, with all your strength, and to love your neighbor as yourself* is worth more than all burnt offerings and sacrifices." And when Jesus saw that he answered with understanding, he said to him, "You are not far from the Kingdom of God."

And no one dared to ask him any more questions.

MARK 12: 28-34

ST. THÉRÈSE OF LISIEUX

"Ah! Lord, I know you don't command the impossible. You know better than I do my weakness and imperfection; You know very well that never would I be able to love my Sisters as You love them, unless You, O my Jesus, loved them in me. *It is because You wanted to give me this grace that You made Your* new commandment. *Oh! How I love this new commandment since it gives me the assurance that Your will is* to love in me *all those You command me to love!" (Story of a Soul,* 221).

REFLECTION

A beautiful element in the spirituality of St. Thérèse is her ability to communicate the Gospel message. In many places in her autobiography she centers her life in love or on humility or on the Cross. Her love for God is evident in her prayerful living, in her desire to imitate Christ and to follow His will as she discerns it in daily living. Her love for neighbor is not without cost as we read in her *Story of a Soul.* She knows that loving those who are difficult to love is a sign of Christian maturity. There is no living with "cheap grace," that is, grace without the Cross, grace without conversion, grace without centering one's life in following Jesus Christ. St. Thérèse understood clearly the meaning of Christian love. As the Lord taught, love for God and for neighbor places us near to the Kingdom of God.

PRAYER

Gracious and loving God, help us to do your will in the push and pull of everyday life. Help us to center our hearts in you, so that we may be faithful to you as was your Son, Jesus Christ the Lord. Amen.

GOSPEL

Jesus addressed this parable to those who were convinced of their own righteousness and despised everyone else. "Two people went up to the temple area to pray; one was a Pharisee and the other was a tax collector. The Pharisee took up his position and spoke this prayer to himself, 'O God, I thank you that I am not like the rest of humanity—greedy, dishonest, adulterous—or even like this tax collector. I fast twice a week, and I pay tithes on my whole income.' But the tax collector stood off at a distance and would not even raise his eyes to heaven but beat his breast and prayed, 'O God, be merciful to me a sinner.' I tell you, the latter went home justified, not the former; for everyone who exalts himself will be humbled, and the one who humbles himself will be exalted."

LUKE 18: 9-14

ST. THÉRÈSE OF LISIEUX

"How will this 'story of a little white flower' come to an end? Perhaps the little flower will be plucked in her youthful freshness or else transplanted to other shores. I don't know, but what I am certain about is that God's Mercy will accompany her always, that it will never cease blessing the dear Mother who offered her to Jesus; she will rejoice eternally at being one of the flowers of her crown. And with this dear Mother she will sing eternally the new canticle of love" (Story of a Soul, 181–82).

REFLECTION

Notice the difference in attitude between the arrogance of the Pharisee and the humility of St. Thérèse. The Pharisee boasts that he is not like the rest of humanity for he has always done wondrous things! St. Thérèse on the other hand sees her life and her crown solely as the consequence of God's continual mercy.

St. Thérèse always had great devotion to the merciful love of God. She viewed God's mercy as much more prominent than God's justice. Her experience told her that she had no reason to fear God. So, we remember . . . God has mercy on those who are merciful in life.

PRAYER

Let us pray.

Loving God, may we always be mindful of your mercy toward us who are sinners. We can always turn to you in confidence like the tax collector who showed humility and honesty before God. We make our prayer through Christ our Lord. Amen.

FOURTH WEEK
OF
LENT

GOSPEL

As Jesus passed by he saw a man blind from birth. His disciples asked him, "Rabbi, who sinned, this man or his parents, that he was born blind?" Jesus answered, "Neither he nor his parents sinned; it is so that the works of God might be made visible through him. We have to do the works of the one who sent me while it is day. Night is coming when no one can work. While I am in the world, I am the light of the world." When he had said this, he spat on the ground and made clay with the saliva, and smeared the clay on his eyes, and said to him, "Go wash in the Pool of Siloam" —which means Sent. So he went and washed, and came back able to see.

His neighbors and those who had seen him earlier as a beggar said, "Isn't this the one who used to sit and beg?" Some said, "It is," but others said, "No, he just looks like him." He said, "I am." So they said to him, "How were your eyes opened?" He replied, "The man called Jesus made clay and anointed my eyes and told me, 'Go to Siloam and wash.' So I went there and washed and was able to see." And they said to him, "Where is he?" He said, "I don't know."

They brought the one who was once blind to the Pharisees. Now Jesus had made clay and opened his eyes on a sabbath. So then the Pharisees also asked him how he was able to see. He said to them, "He put clay on my eyes, and I washed, and now I can see." So some of the Pharisees said, "This man is not from God, because he does not keep the sabbath." But others said, "How can a sinful man do such signs?" And there was a division among them. So they said to the blind man again, "What do you have to say about him, since he opened your eyes?" He said, "He is a prophet."

Now the Jews did not believe that he had been blind and gained his sight until they summoned the parents of the one who had gained his sight. They asked them, "Is this your son, who you say was born blind? How does he now see?" His parents answered and said, "We know that this is our son and that he was born blind. We do not know how he sees now, nor do we know who opened his eyes. Ask him, he is of age; he can speak for himself." His parents said this because they were afraid of the Jews, for the Jews had already agreed that if anyone acknowledged him as the Christ, he would be expelled from the synagogue. For this reason his parents said, "He is of age; question him."

So a second time they called the man who had been blind and said to him, "Give God the praise! We know that this man is a sinner." He replied, "If he is a sinner, I do not know. One thing I do know is that I was blind and now I see." So they said to him, "What did he do to you? How did he open your eyes?" He answered them, "I told you already and you did not listen. Why do you want to hear it again? Do you want to become his disciples, too?" They ridiculed him and said, "You are that man's disciple; we are disciples of Moses! We know that God spoke to Moses, but we do not know where this one is from." The man answered and said to them, "This is what is so amazing, that you do not know where he is from, yet he opened my eyes. We know that God does not listen to sinners, but if one is devout and does his will, he listens to him. It is unheard of that anyone ever opened the eyes of a person born blind. If this man were not from God, he would not be able to do anything." They answered and said to him, "You were born totally in sin, and are you trying to teach us?" Then they threw him out.

When Jesus heard that they had thrown him out, he found him and said, "Do you believe in the Son of Man?" He answered and said, "Who is he, sir, that I may believe in him?" Jesus said to him, "You have seen him, the one speaking with you is he." He said, "I do believe, Lord," and he worshiped him. Then Jesus said, "I came into this world for judgment, so that those who do not see might see, and those who do see might become blind."

Some of the Pharisees who were with him heard this and said to him, "Surely we are not also blind, are we?" Jesus said to them, "If you were blind, you would have no sin; but now you are saying, 'We see,' so your sin remains."

JOHN 9: 1-41

Shorter form: JOHN 9:1, 6-9, 13-17, 34-38
Longer form may be optionally read on any day in the fourth week of Lent

ST. THÉRÈSE OF LISIEUX

"It seems to me that if a little flower could speak, it would tell simply what God has done for it without trying to hide its blessings. It would not say, under the pretext of a false humility, it is not beautiful or without perfume, that the sun has taken away its splendor or the storm has broken its stem when it knows that all this is untrue. The flower about to tell her story rejoices at having to publish the totally gratuitous gifts of Jesus" (Story of a Soul, 15).

REFLECTION

In both the Gospel and in the passage from St. Thérèse we find a common conviction: God who is good can do great things for us. The motive is God's love. In the case of the blind man, he is cured and is able to see and he comes to profess faith in Jesus. In St. Thérèse we find a story of God's continual blessings in her life. Both stories should give us confidence in God's power to bring about new life in us. Fundamental to our relationship to God is faith in Him. We need to trust in His presence and in His loving care for us.

St. Thérèse went through a final period in her life when she was assailed by temptations against her belief in heaven. She claimed to have made more acts of faith in the last year of her life than at any time previously. She wrote that even though she did not experience the joy of faith, she still made every effort to do its works. She would not let herself be done in by doubts. Our lives need to be grounded in a strong faith in God, trust in God's saving presence.

PRAYER

Let us pray.

Loving Father, may we awaken to your presence in our lives and help us to follow your way to holiness of life. Heal us of our infirmities. We ask this through Christ our Lord. Amen.

GOSPEL

JESUS SAID TO NICODEMUS:

"Just as Moses lifted up the serpent in the desert, so must the Son of Man be lifted up, so that everyone who believes in him may have eternal life."

For God so loved the world that he gave his only Son, so that everyone who believes in him might not perish but might have eternal life. For God did not send his Son into the world to condemn the world, but that the world might be saved through him. Whoever believes in him will not be condemned, but whoever does not believe has already been condemned, because he has not believed in the name of the only Son of God. And this is the verdict, that the light came into the world, but people preferred darkness to light, because their works were evil. For everyone who does wicked things hates the light and does not come toward the light, so that his works might not be exposed. But whoever lives the truth comes to the light, so that his works may be clearly seen as done in God.

JOHN 3: 14-21

ST. THÉRÈSE OF LISIEUX

"My soul soon shared in the sufferings of my heart. Spiritual aridity was my daily bread and, deprived of all consolation, I was still the happiest of creatures since all my desires had been satisfied" (Story of a Soul, 157).

REFLECTION

St. Thérèse always sought to live the truth, that is, the truth of Gospel living. As today's Gospel proclaims, to live the truth means to come into the light. Light accompanies a life of integrity. Even though St. Thérèse experienced suffering and aridity, at a deeper level she lived happily and in peace. She desired above all to give her life to Jesus as a way to serve the needs of sinners and of priests. She saw that deep desire being fulfilled, beginning with the conversion of the murderer Henri Pranzini (see *Story of a Soul*, 99–100) and continuing in her prayer and sacrifice for priests. Her very life was a journey into the light of Christ. Her heart sang a song of dedication.

The Christian community is called to live the truth of the Gospel. True light appears in absorbing the Gospel values. Peace comes in living in the light.

PRAYER

Let us pray.

Father, bring each one of us into the light of your truth. May we experience the light of Christ by offering our very lives to the God who loves each one of us. We make our prayer through Christ our Lord. Amen.

GOSPEL

Tax collectors and sinners were all drawing near to listen to Jesus, but the Pharisees and scribes began to complain, saying, "This man welcomes sinners and eats with them."

So to them Jesus addressed this parable: "A man had two sons, and the younger son said to his father, 'Father, give me the share of your estate that should come to me.' So the father divided the property between them. After a few days, the younger son collected all his belongings and set off to a distant country where he squandered his inheritance on a life of dissipation. When he had freely spent everything, a severe famine struck that country, and he found himself in dire need. So he hired himself out to one of the local citizens who sent him to his farm to tend the swine. And he longed to eat his fill of the pods on which the swine fed, but nobody gave him any. Coming to his senses he thought, 'How many of my father's hired workers have more than enough food to eat, but here am I, dying from hunger. I shall get up and go to my father and I shall say to him, "Father, I have sinned against heaven and against you. I no longer deserve to be called your son; treat me as you would treat one of your hired workers."' So he got up and went back to his father. While he was still a long way off, his father caught sight of him, and was filled with compassion. He ran to his son, embraced him and kissed him. His son said to him, 'Father, I have sinned against heaven and against you; I no longer deserve to be called your son.' But his father ordered his servants, 'Quickly, bring the finest robe and put it on him; put a ring on his finger and sandals on his feet. Take the fattened calf and slaughter it. Then let us celebrate with a feast, because this son of mine was dead, and has come to life again; he was lost, and has been found.' Then the celebration began. Now the older son had been out in the field and, on his way back, as he neared the house, he heard the sound of music and dancing. He called one of the servants and asked what this might mean. The servant said to him, 'Your brother has returned and your father has slaughtered the fattened calf because he has him back safe and sound.' He became angry, and when he refused to enter the house, his father came out and pleaded with him. He said to his father in reply, 'Look, all these years I served you and not once did I disobey your orders; yet you never gave me even a young goat to feast on with my friends. But when your son returns who swallowed up your property with prostitutes, for him you slaughter the fattened calf.' He said to him, 'My son, you are here with me always; everything I have is yours. But now we must celebrate and rejoice, because your brother was dead and has come to life again; he was lost and has been found.'"

LUKE 15: 1-3, 11-32

ST. THÉRÈSE OF LISIEUX

"How merciful is the way God has guided me. Never has He given me the desire for anything which He has not given me, and even His bitter chalice seemed delightful to me" (Story of a Soul, 152).

REFLECTION

The mercy of God is recognizable in both the story of the Prodigal Son and in St. Thérèse. The Prodigal Son tried to find meaning in serving his desire for pleasure. He found that it was fleeting and without depth. He then experienced God's mercy in his desire to return home, to return to the familiar and the secure. St. Thérèse saw her whole life embraced by God's mercy. His mercy enabled her to accept adversity as well as blessings. Mercy is a virtue calling us to serve others through compassion, empathy, forgiveness, and self-emptying love.

PRAYER

Let us pray.

Gracious God, help us to live according to the truth of the Gospel. Keep us from wandering off the path marked by faith, hope, and love. We make our prayer though Christ our Lord. Amen.

GOSPEL

At that time Jesus left [Samaria] for Galilee. For Jesus himself testified that a prophet has no honor in his native place. When he came into Galilee, the Galileans welcomed him, since they had seen all he had done in Jerusalem at the feast; for they themselves had gone to the feast.

Then he returned to Cana in Galilee, where he had made the water wine. Now there was a royal official whose son was ill in Capernaum. When he heard that Jesus had arrived in Galilee from Judea, he went to him and asked him to come down and heal his son, who was near death. Jesus said to him, "Unless you people see signs and wonders, you will not believe." The royal official said to him, "Sir, come down before my child dies." Jesus said to him, "You may go; your son will live." The man believed what Jesus said to him and left. While the man was on his way back, his slaves met him and told him that his boy would live. He asked them when he began to recover. They told him, "The fever left him yesterday, about one in the afternoon." The father realized that just at that time Jesus had said to him, "Your son will live," and he and his whole household came to believe. Now this was the second sign Jesus did when he came to Galilee from Judea.

JOHN 4: 43-54

ST. THÉRÈSE OF LISIEUX

A letter of St. Thérèse to her cousin Celine Maudelonde: *"I feel, dear little friend, that I can speak freely to you; you understand the language of faith better than that of the world, and the Jesus of your First Communion has remained the Master of your heart. . . . It is because of Him that your love is so tender and so strong" (The Letters of St. Thérèse, vol. 2, 865).*

REFLECTION

The importance of faith appears in both readings. Without faith it is impossible to have a relationship to God. The royal official believed in Jesus' word of healing and indeed his son was made well. St. Thérèse's letter indicates that her cousin Celine has a strong love for others because of her commitment to Jesus in faith.

The question arises in our own experience: How strong is our faith in Jesus Christ? Does faith make a difference in the way we live? Are we confident that Jesus can touch our lives and move us to seek a more generous heart? Do we seek to know Christ through our prayerful reading of Scripture? Perhaps we need to let go of our self preoccupation and seek God's will in faith, hope, and love. It will make all the difference in the world.

PRAYER

Let us pray.

Lord, our God, help us to turn to you with the confidence that comes through faith. We want to follow you each day but we need the strength that only your grace can provide. We make our prayer through Christ our Lord. Amen.

GOSPEL

There was a feast of the Jews, and Jesus went up to Jerusalem. Now there is in Jerusalem at the Sheep Gate a pool called in Hebrew Bethesda, with five porticoes. In these lay a large number of ill, blind, lame, and crippled. One man was there who had been ill for thirty-eight years. When Jesus saw him lying there and knew that he had been ill for a long time, he said to him, "Do you want to be well?" The sick man answered him, "Sir, I have no one to put me into the pool when the water is stirred up; while I am on my way, someone else gets down there before me." Jesus said to him, "Rise, take up your mat, and walk." Immediately the man became well, took up his mat, and walked.

Now that day was a sabbath. So the Jews said to the man who was cured, "It is the sabbath, and it is not lawful for you to carry your mat." He answered them, "The man who made me well told me, 'Take up your mat and walk.'" They asked him, "Who is the man who told you, 'Take it up and walk'?" The man who was healed did not know who it was, for Jesus had slipped away, since there was a crowd there. After this Jesus found him in the temple area and said to him, "Look, you are well; do not sin any more, so that nothing worse may happen to you." The man went and told the Jews that Jesus was the one who had made him well. Therefore, the Jews began to persecute Jesus because he did this on a sabbath.

JOHN 5: 1-16

ST. THÉRÈSE OF LISIEUX

"Well, I am this child, the object of the foreseeing love of a Father *who has not sent His word to save the* just, *but* sinners. *He wants me* to love *Him because He* has forgiven *me not much but ALL.* *He has not expected me to* love Him much *like Mary Magdalene, but He has willed that I KNOW how He has loved me with a love of* unspeakable foresight *in order that now I may love Him unto* folly!*" (Story of a Soul, 84)*.

REFLECTION

Today's Gospel tells the story of a physical cure. Jesus has countless ways of healing our lives. St. Thérèse believes that God has preserved her from obstacles which would have seriously challenged her spiritual life. As a consequence her heart totally belongs to God for God has first loved her. Her love for Jesus will be "unto folly." She believes that God's love within her enables her to love all the Sisters with whom she lives.

Carmelite spirituality is focused upon the character of our love for God and neighbor. What helps us to love well is the grace of God within us, prompting us to let go of antipathies, to be generous with others in their needs and to be gracious as a disciple of Jesus Christ.

PRAYER

Lord, heal us of our prejudices, our hurts, our selfishness. Turn us into faithful disciples of Jesus Christ. We make our prayer through Christ our Lord. Amen.

GOSPEL

Jesus answered the Jews: "My Father is at work until now, so I am at work." For this reason they tried all the more to kill him, because he not only broke the sabbath but he also called God his own father, making himself equal to God.

Jesus answered and said to them, "Amen, amen, I say to you, the Son cannot do anything on his own, but only what he sees the Father doing; for what he does, the Son will do also. For the Father loves the Son and shows him everything that he himself does, and he will show him greater works than these, so that you may be amazed. For just as the Father raises the dead and gives life, so also does the Son give life to whomever he wishes. Nor does the Father judge anyone, but he has given all judgment to the Son, so that all may honor the Son just as they honor the Father. Whoever does not honor the Son does not honor the Father who sent him. Amen, amen, I say to you, whoever hears my word and believes in the one who sent me has eternal life and will not come to condemnation, but has passed from death to life. Amen, amen, I say to you, the hour is coming and is now here when the dead will hear the voice of the Son of God, and those who hear will live. For just as the Father has life in himself, so also he gave to the Son the possession of life in himself. And he gave him power to exercise judgment, because he is the Son of Man. Do not be amazed at this, because the hour is coming in which all who are in the tombs will hear his voice and will come out, those who have done good deeds to the resurrection of life, but those who have done wicked deeds to the resurrection of condemnation.

"I cannot do anything on my own; I judge as I hear, and my judgment is just, because I do not seek my own will but the will of the one who sent me."

JOHN 5: 17-30

ST. THÉRÈSE OF LISIEUX

"I've your heart, your adored Face, Your sweet look that has wounded me. I've the kiss of your sacred mouth, I love you and want nothing more, Jesus" ("The Canticle of Celine" in *The Poetry of St. Thérèse*, 102).

REFLECTION

The Gospel of John tells us that "whoever does not honor the Son does not honor the Father who sent him." That is simply because of the union between the Father and the Son. Wherever the Son is, there is the Father and the Holy Spirit. The Trinity surrounds us with a saving love.

We find a sense of passionate love for God in St. Thérèse's poem. Jesus is all. She does not need to seize anything or anyone with a sense of ultimate meaning.

Our struggle often enough is maintaining a consistent pattern of relationship to God . . . in daily prayer, virtuous living, in an engaging sacramental life. The tradition refers to a problem called "acedia," which is laziness in regard to our relationship to the Lord. The Lenten period can help us to return to God with all our hearts. It begins by being mindful of God's presence in our lives in the ordinary and the everyday.

PRAYER

Let us pray.

Loving Father, we ask you to help us to be mindful of you each day by offering to you our daily prayer and a life of integrity. Enable us to overcome any apathy or indifference in our love for you. We make our prayer through Christ our Lord. Amen.

GOSPEL

JESUS SAID TO THE JEWS:

"If I testify on my own behalf, my testimony is not true. But there is another who testifies on my behalf, and I know that the testimony he gives on my behalf is true. You sent emissaries to John, and he testified to the truth. I do not accept human testimony, but I say this so that you may be saved. He was a burning and shining lamp, and for a while you were content to rejoice in his light. But I have testimony greater than John's. The works that the Father gave me to accomplish, these works that I perform testify on my behalf that the Father has sent me. Moreover, the Father who sent me has testified on my behalf. But you have never heard his voice nor seen his form, and you do not have his word remaining in you, because you do not believe in the one whom he has sent. You search the Scriptures, because you think you have eternal life through them; even they testify on my behalf. But you do not want to come to me to have life.

"I do not accept human praise; moreover, I know that you do not have the love of God in you. I came in the name of my Father, but you do not accept me; yet if another comes in his own name, you will accept him. How can you believe, when you accept praise from one another and do not seek the praise that comes from the only God? Do not think that I will accuse you before the Father: the one who will accuse you is Moses, in whom you have placed your hope. For if you had believed Moses, you would have believed me, because he wrote about me. But if you do not believe his writings, how will you believe my words?"

JOHN 5: 31-47

ST. THÉRÈSE OF LISIEUX

"Oh my Jesus, I love you! I love the Church, my Mother! I recall that 'the smallest act of PURE LOVE *is of more value to her than all other* works together.' *But is* PURE LOVE *in my heart? Are my measureless desires only but a dream, a folly? Ah! If this be so, Jesus, then enlighten me, for You know I am seeking only the truth"* (Story of a Soul, 197).

REFLECTION

John the Baptist testified to the truth. Indeed, he prepared the way of the Lord. The truth of the Gospel is that Jesus is the Son of God and shows us the way to the Father.

St. Thérèse wishes to live her life in testimony to the truth of Jesus Christ. Her limitless desires to offer to the Lord only pure love seem to her to be grounded in truth. Her little way of love has blossomed as a valid expression of Gospel life. She is among us as a Doctor of the Church.

Our testimony on behalf of Jesus rings true when it is expressed in love and seeks no recompense. Our Christian witness will help to bring about the new creation.

PRAYER

Let us pray.

God, our Father, help us in bearing witness to Jesus. May our love be pure and generous in the service of our Church and our world. We ask this through Christ our Lord. Amen.

GOSPEL

Jesus moved about within Galilee; he did not wish to travel in Judea, because the Jews were trying to kill him. But the Jewish feast of Tabernacles was near.

But when his brothers had gone up to the feast, he himself also went up, not openly but as it were in secret.

Some of the inhabitants of Jerusalem said, "Is he not the one they are trying to kill? And look, he is speaking openly and they say nothing to him. Could the authorities have realized that he is the Christ? But we know where he is from. When the Christ comes, no one will know where he is from." So Jesus cried out in the temple area as he was teaching and said, "You know me and also know where I am from. Yet I did not come on my own, but the one who sent me, whom you do not know, is true. I know him, because I am from him, and he sent me." So they tried to arrest him, but no one laid a hand upon him, because his hour had not yet come.

JOHN 7: 1-2, 10, 25-30

ST. THÉRÈSE OF LISIEUX

"Dear little Sister, do not be a sad little girl when seeing you are not understood, that you are judged badly, that you are forgotten, but lay a trap for everybody by taking care to do like others, or rather by doing for yourself what others are doing for you, that is, forget all that is not Jesus, forget yourself for His love!" (The Letters of St. Thérèse, vol. 2, 1138).

REFLECTION

The Gospel of John announces that there exists a real threat to Jesus' life. However, Jesus does not hide from expressing the truth about his identity. He proclaims his relationship to the Father in spite of the animosity toward him.

St. Thérèse's letter is addressed to Sister Marie of Jesus. Her advice to Sister Marie calls for a spiritual maturity that she may not yet possess. "Forget all that is not Jesus." Yet, St. Thérèse is making a very valid observation. The attention of others can be very fleeting or possessive or immature or sinful. St. Thérèse would have us center our lives in love for Jesus Christ, the only relationship that brings true joy.

PRAYER

Let us pray.

Lord, enable me to center my life in your love and to be a witness to your presence in our world. We ask this through Christ our Lord. Amen.

GOSPEL

Some in the crowd who heard these words of Jesus said, "This is truly the Prophet." Others said, "This is the Christ." But others said, "The Christ will not come from Galilee, will he? Does not Scripture say that the Christ will be of David's family and come from Bethlehem, the village where David lived?" So a division occurred in the crowd because of him. Some of them even wanted to arrest him, but no one laid hands on him.

So the guards went to the chief priests and Pharisees, who asked them, "Why did you not bring him?" The guards answered, "Never before has anyone spoken like this man." So the Pharisees answered them, "Have you also been deceived? Have any of the authorities or the Pharisees believed in him? But this crowd, which does not know the law, is accursed." Nicodemus, one of their members who had come to him earlier, said to them, "Does our law condemn a man before it first hears him and finds out what he is doing?" They answered and said to him, "You are not from Galilee also, are you? Look and see that no prophet arises from Galilee."

Then each went to his own house.

JOHN 7: 40-53

ST. THÉRÈSE OF LISIEUX

"Ah! In spite of my littleness, I would like to enlighten souls as did the Prophets *and the* Doctors*" (Story of a Soul, 192).*

It is important to understand that St. Thérèse thinks of her littleness not as an inferior state of being but simply as the situation of one who in her mind cannot accomplish the magnificent gestures of mortification and charity that were the lot of the great saints. Her "little way" became an alternative form of holiness of life and indeed one that can be embraced by all people.

118

REFLECTION

Jesus was considered a prophet, one who spoke with authority about relationship to God. St. Thérèse would wish to do something similar, to speak about God and God's saving love to every corner of the world. And she desired to preach until the end of time.

How much enthusiasm do we have to make God known? Do we know how we would evangelize? A very good way to begin would be by living a life of integrity. In doing so we would provide a model for discipleship of Jesus Christ.

Often enough lives are wasted in fostering idols which do not satisfy with any amount of ultimate fulfillment. Possessions, careers, power and position are some idols which have adherents in our society. Yet, true evangelization would alert us to view all things in relationship to Jesus who saves us from the sadness which idol making creates.

PRAYER

Let us pray.

Lord, I want to follow you in integrity of life. Warm my heart so that I may seek the wisdom in your word in Scripture. Help me to discern the true from the false, the real from illusion. We make our prayer through Christ our Lord. Amen.

FIFTH WEEK
OF
LENT

GOSPEL

Now a man was ill, Lazarus from Bethany, the village of Mary and her sister Martha. Mary was the one who had anointed the Lord with perfumed oil and dried his feet with her hair; it was her brother Lazarus who was ill. So the sisters sent word to Jesus saying, "Master, the one you love is ill." When Jesus heard this he said, "This illness is not to end in death, but is for the glory of God, that the Son of God may be glorified through it." Now Jesus loved Martha and her sister and Lazarus. So when he heard that he was ill, he remained for two days in the place where he was. Then after this he said to his disciples, "Let us go back to Judea." The disciples said to him, "Rabbi, the Jews were just trying to stone you, and you want to go back there?" Jesus answered, "Are there not twelve hours in a day? If one walks during the day, he does not stumble, because he sees the light of this world. But if one walks at night, he stumbles, because the light is not in him." He said this, and then told them, "Our friend Lazarus is asleep, but I am going to awaken him." So the disciples said to him, "Master, if he is asleep, he will be saved." But Jesus was talking about his death, while they thought that he meant ordinary sleep. So then Jesus said to them clearly, "Lazarus has died. And I am glad for you that I was not there, that you may believe. Let us go to him." So Thomas, called Didymus, said to his fellow disciples, "Let us also go to die with him."

When Jesus arrived, he found that Lazarus had already been in the tomb for four days. Now Bethany was near Jerusalem, only about two miles away. And many of the Jews had come to Martha and Mary to comfort them about their brother. When Martha heard that Jesus was coming, she went to meet him; but Mary sat at home. Martha said to Jesus, "Lord, if you had been here, my brother would not have died. But even now I know that whatever you ask of God, God will give you."

Jesus said to her, "Your brother will rise." Martha said to him, "I know he will rise, in the resurrection on the last day." Jesus told her, "I am the resurrection and the life; whoever believes in me, even if he dies, will live, and everyone who lives and believes in me will never die. Do you believe this?" She said to him, "Yes, Lord. I have come to believe that you are the Christ, the Son of God, the one who is coming into the world."

When she had said this, she went and called her sister Mary secretly, saying, "The teacher is here and is asking for you." As soon as she heard this, she rose quickly and went to him. For Jesus had not yet come into the village, but was still where Martha had met him. So when the Jews who were with her in the house comforting her saw Mary get up quickly and go out, they followed her, presuming that she was going to the tomb to weep there. When Mary came to where Jesus was and saw him, she fell at his feet and said to him, "Lord, if you had been here, my brother would not have died." When Jesus saw her weeping and the Jews who had come with her weeping, he became perturbed and deeply troubled, and said, "Where have you laid him?" They said to him, "Sir, come and see." And Jesus wept. So the Jews said, "See how he loved him." But some of them said, "Could not the one who opened the eyes of the blind man have done something so that this man would not have died?"

So Jesus, perturbed again, came to the tomb. It was a cave, and a stone lay across it. Jesus said, "Take away the stone." Martha, the dead man's sister, said to him, "Lord, by now there will be a stench; he has been dead for four days." Jesus said to her, "Did I not tell you that if you believe you will see the glory of God?" So they took away the stone. And Jesus raised his eyes and said, "Father, I thank you for hearing me. I know that you always hear me; but because of the crowd here I have said this, that they may believe that you sent me." And when he had said this, he cried out in a loud voice, "Lazarus, come out!" The dead man came out, tied hand and foot with burial bands, and his face was wrapped in a cloth. So Jesus said to them, "Untie him and let him go."

Now many of the Jews who had come to Mary and seen what he had done began to believe in him.

JOHN 11: 1-45

Shorter form: JOHN 11:3-7, 17, 20-27, 33b-45
Longer form may be optionally read on any day in the fifth week of Lent

ST. THÉRÈSE OF LISIEUX

"It seems to me that if a little flower could speak, it would tell simply what God has done for it without trying to hide its blessings. . . .The flower about to tell her story rejoices at having to publish the totally gratuitous gifts of Jesus. She knows that nothing in herself was capable of attracting the divine glances, and His mercy alone brought about everything that is good in her" (Story of a Soul, 15).

REFLECTION

Jesus' presence to us creates new life. Lazarus came out of the tomb. St. Thérèse acknowledges that her life became an offering to Jesus as she views it through the mercy of God. Every good thing comes from God.

Yet there is great suffering in our world. We are subject to the limitations and troubles that come with the human condition. But new life is always possible . . . through reconciliation, through conversion of life from sin to virtue, through renewed commitment. Selfishness is the enemy of life; self-emptying love is life's fulfillment.

PRAYER

Let us pray.

Loving God, we ask that you bring our lives into conformity with your will for us. We wish to be your true disciples and to witness to your love in our world. We make our prayer through Christ our Lord. Amen.

GOSPEL

Some Greeks who had come to worship at the Passover Feast came to Philip, who was from Bethsaida in Galilee, and asked him, "Sir, we would like to see Jesus." Philip went and told Andrew; then Andrew and Philip went and told Jesus. Jesus answered them, "The hour has come for the Son of Man to be glorified. Amen, amen, I say to you, unless a grain of wheat falls to the ground and dies, it remains just a grain of wheat; but if it dies, it produces much fruit. Whoever loves his life loses it, and whoever hates his life in this world will preserve it for eternal life. Whoever serves me must follow me, and where I am, there also will my servant be. The Father will honor whoever serves me.

"I am troubled now. Yet what should I say? 'Father, save me from this hour'? But it was for this purpose that I came to this hour. Father, glorify your name." Then a voice came from heaven, "I have glorified it and will glorify it again." The crowd there heard it and said it was thunder; but others said, "An angel has spoken to him." Jesus answered and said, "This voice did not come for my sake but for yours. Now is the time of judgement on this world; now the ruler of this world will be driven out. And when I am lifted up from the earth, I will draw everyone to myself." He said this indicating the kind of death he would die.

JOHN 12: 20-33

ST. THÉRÈSE OF LISIEUX

"I really feel that I would have no disappointment, for when one expects pure and unmixed suffering, the smallest joy becomes an unhoped-for surprise. And you know, Mother, that suffering itself becomes the greatest of joys when one seeks it as the most precious of treasures" (Story of a Soul, 218).

REFLECTION

Such a hope filled exclamation from Jesus! "And when I am lifted up from the earth, I will draw everyone to myself." We are born for union with God. Eternal life is our destiny and Jesus provides the way to the eternal shore through his grace.

St. Thérèse saw that life in the world is fraught with suffering. She sees a need to embrace suffering as Jesus did. This openness to suffering she calls "the most precious of treasures." She is not suggesting that suffering is to be loved for its own sake. What she intends is that our suffering is a means of identifying more with Christ who gave his life for us. The dying and rising pattern of life creates a deep union with Jesus.

PRAYER

Let us pray.

God, You who are gracious and loving, enable us to walk with you on the road to Calvary. Your love can fill our heart so that our commitment to you is full of integrity and truth. We make our prayer through Christ our Lord. Amen.

GOSPEL

Jesus went to the Mount of Olives. But early in the morning he arrived again in the temple area, and all the people started coming to him, and he sat down and taught them. Then the scribes and the Pharisees brought a woman who had been caught in adultery and made her stand in the middle. They said to him, "Teacher, this woman was caught in the very act of committing adultery. Now in the law, Moses commanded us to stone such women. So what do you say?" They said this to test him, so that they could have some charge to bring against him. Jesus bent down and began to write on the ground with his finger. But when they continued asking him, he straightened up and said to them, "Let the one among you who is without sin be the first to throw a stone at her." Again he bent down and wrote on the ground. And in response, they went away one by one, beginning with the elders. So he was left alone with the woman before him. Then Jesus straightened up and said to her, "Woman, where are they? Has no one condemned you?" She replied, "No one, sir." Then Jesus said, "Neither do I condemn you. Go, and from now on do not sin any more."

JOHN 8: 1-11

ST. THÉRÈSE OF LISIEUX

"To me the Lord has always been merciful and good, slow to anger and abounding in steadfast love" (Psalm 102:8, *Story of a Soul*, 15).

REFLECTION

How could anyone fear a God who is merciful love? We see the love of God present in Jesus' concern for the woman caught in adultery. She was called to conversion and new life. "Go, and from now on do not sin anymore."

St. Thérèse frequently referred to the mercy of God. At the very end of her *Story of a Soul* she wrote, "Yes, I feel it; even though I had on my conscience all the sins that can be committed, I would go, my heart broken with sorrow, and throw myself into Jesus' arms, for I know how much He loves the prodigal child who returns to Him" (259). Her very engaging sense of God's merciful love stood in contrast to the prevailing emphasis on God who is the judge of our lives. While we are morally responsible for our actions, God calls us to continual conversion. All the saints passed through purifications in order to experience deeper union with God. The work of God's grace in our lives is to communicate God's love for us.

PRAYER

Let us pray.

O God, have mercy on me a sinner. Help me to hear your call to holiness of life amid the challenges I must face in a broken world. May I know the peace that is your gift. We make our prayer through Christ our Lord. Amen.

GOSPEL

Jesus went to the Mount of Olives. But early in the morning he arrived again in the temple area, and all the people started coming to him, and he sat down and taught them. Then the scribes and the Pharisees brought a woman who had been caught in adultery and made her stand in the middle. They said to him, "Teacher, this woman was caught in the very act of committing adultery. Now in the law, Moses commanded us to stone such women. So what do you say?" They said this to test him, so that they could have some charge to bring against him. Jesus bent down and began to write on the ground with his finger. But when they continued asking him, he straightened up and said to them, "Let the one among you who is without sin be the first to throw a stone at her." Again he bent down and wrote on the ground. And in response, they went away one by one, beginning with the elders. So he was left alone with the woman before him. Then Jesus straightened up and said to her, "Woman, where are they? Has no one condemned you?" She replied, "No one, sir." Then Jesus said, "Neither do I condemn you. Go, and from now on do not sin any more."

JOHN 8: 1-11

ST. THÉRÈSE OF LISIEUX

"I felt in the depths of my heart certain *that our desires would be granted, but to obtain courage to pray for sinners I told God I was sure He would pardon the poor, unfortunate Pranzini; that I'd believed this even if he went to his death without* any signs of repentance *or without* having gone to confession. *I was absolutely confident in the mercy of Jesus. But I was begging him for a 'sign' of repentance only for my own simple consolation" (Story of a Soul,* 100).

REFLECTION

Jesus makes clear that no one is without sin. All those men who had gathered to stone the adulteress left and Jesus assures her of forgiveness and asks her not to sin anymore.

St. Thérèse was aware of the story of a murderer by the name of Pranzini. He had killed a woman and her daughter and was condemned to death in 1887. As he was about to be guillotined, Pranzini, in a final moment, seized the cross a priest was holding and kissed the sacred wounds three times. St. Thérèse saw this gesture as a sign of repentance and she rejoiced. As she wrote, "his soul went to receive the merciful sentence of Him who declares that in heaven there will be more joy over one sinner who does penance that over ninety-nine just who have no need of repentance" (*Story of a Soul*, 100).

St. Thérèse lived her whole life conscious of God's mercy. Thus, her demeanor was always full of confidence and hope.

PRAYER

Let us pray.

God of all consolation, help each one of us to seek your forgiveness for our sins. May we celebrate your merciful presence among us. We ask this through Christ our Lord. Amen.

In Year C, when the preceding Gospel is read on Sunday, the following text is used.

GOSPEL

Jesus spoke to them again, saying, "I am the light of the world. Whoever follows me will not walk in darkness, but will have the light of life." So the Pharisees said to him, "You testify on your own behalf, so your testimony cannot be verified." Jesus answered and said to them, "Even if I do testify on my own behalf, my testimony can be verified, because I know where I came from and where I am going. But you do not know where I come from or where I am going. You judge by appearances, but I do not judge anyone. And even if I should judge, my judgment is valid, because I am not alone, but it is I and the Father who sent me. Even in your law it is written that the testimony of two men can be verified. I testify on my behalf and so does the Father who sent me." So they said to him, "Where is your father?" Jesus answered, "You know neither me nor my Father. If you knew me, you would know my Father also." He spoke these words while teaching in the treasury in the temple area. But no one arrested him, because his hour had not yet come.

JOHN 8: 12-20

ST. THÉRÈSE OF LISIEUX

"On that night of light *began the third period of my life, the most beautiful and the most filled with graces from heaven. The work I had been unable to do in ten years was done by Jesus in one instant, contenting himself with my good will which was never lacking" (Story of a Soul, 98).*

REFLECTION

Jesus was sent into the world by the Father in order to communicate truth about ourselves, to reveal the Father's love for us and to bring us to salvation. The Gospel challenges us to come to know Jesus and the Father. Familiarity with the gospels enables us to know Jesus and to come to love Him more deeply.

St. Thérèse celebrates God's grace that came to her through Jesus Christ. She knew that she was overly sensitive and spoiled. On Christmas Eve in 1886 she experienced the grace of her conversion to which the above quotation refers. In an instant, she felt charity enter her soul. The truth is that her excessive sensitivity left her. She was no longer troubled by too much self-focus. Once she entered the Carmel of Lisieux (April 9, 1888), St. Thérèse manifested a generous and loving heart. She never sought any special attention and offered her life for sinners and for priests.

St. Thérèse believed that a contemplative life of silence and hidden virtue offered to Jesus Christ could mediate greatness to the Church.

PRAYER

Let us pray.

O God, urge us by your grace to come to know and to love you profoundly. May we be true disciples and manifest God's love in our lives. We make our prayer through Christ our Lord. Amen.

GOSPEL

JESUS SAID TO THE PHARISEES:

"I am going away and you will look for me, but you will die in your sin. Where I am going you cannot come." So the Jews said, "He is not going to kill himself, is he, because he said, 'Where I am going you cannot come'?" He said to them, "You belong to what is below, I belong to what is above. You belong to this world, but I do not belong to this world. That is why I told you that you will die in your sins. For if you do not believe that I AM, you will die in your sins." So they said to him, "Who are you?" Jesus said to them, "What I told you from the beginning. I have much to say about you in condemnation. But the one who sent me is true, and what I heard from him I tell the world." They did not realize that he was speaking to them of the Father. So Jesus said to them, "When you lift up the Son of Man, then you will realize that I AM, and that I do nothing on my own, but I say only what the Father taught me. The one who sent me is with me. He has not left me alone, because I always do what is pleasing to him." Because he spoke this way, many came to believe in him.

JOHN 8: 21-30

ST. THÉRÈSE OF LISIEUX

"All the great truths of religion, the mysteries of eternity, plunged my soul into a state of joy not of the earth. I experienced already what God reserved for those who love Him (not with the eye but with the heart), and seeing the eternal rewards had no proportion to life's small sacrifices, I wanted to love, to love Jesus with a passion, giving Him a thousand proofs of my love while it was possible" (Story of a Soul, 102).

REFLECTION

Jesus accomplished what was pleasing to the Father. St. Thérèse, as a disciple of Jesus, expresses a consuming passion to love Jesus with every fiber of her being. She simply wanted to please God in everything. Her total commitment to Jesus in Carmel is patently obvious.

How is it possible to develop a Christian commitment akin to St. Thérèse of Lisieux? Only through the grace of God which moves us to pray often, to be open to God's presence in our world, to value the dignity of others and to grow in virtue throughout our life.

Part of the process of living an authentic spiritual life means turning away from idols we create . . . possessions, a particular person, a career . . . in order that our hearts can become centered in Jesus Christ. There is some struggle involved because our hearts are restless, as St. Augustine wrote, and conversion to the love of God involves a lifetime.

PRAYER

Let us pray.

Loving God, move my heart so that I may center my life in you. I want to do your will and to witness to your goodness in my life. Do not let me wander from your love. We make our prayer through Christ our Lord. Amen.

GOSPEL

Jesus said to those Jews who believed in him, "If you remain in my word, you will truly be my disciples, and you will know the truth, and the truth will set you free." They answered him, "We are descendants of Abraham and have never been enslaved to anyone. How can you say, 'You will become free'?" Jesus answered them, "Amen, amen, I say to you, everyone who commits sin is a slave of sin. A slave does not remain in a household forever, but a son always remains. So if the Son frees you, then you will truly be free. I know that you are descendants of Abraham. But you are trying to kill me, because my word has no room among you. I tell you what I have seen in the Father's presence; then do what you have heard from the Father."

They answered and said to him, "Our father is Abraham." Jesus said to them, "If you were Abraham's children, you would be doing the works of Abraham. But now you are trying to kill me, a man who has told you the truth that I heard from God; Abraham did not do this. You are doing the works of your father!" So they said to him, "We were not born of fornication. We have one Father, God." Jesus said to them, "If God were your Father, you would love me, for I came from God and am here; I did not come on my own, but he sent me."

JOHN 8: 31-42

ST. THÉRÈSE OF LISIEUX

"O Divine Word! You are the Adored Eagle whom I love and who alone attracts me! *Coming into this land of exile, You willed to suffer and to die in order* to draw *souls to the bosom of the Eternal Fire of the Blessed Trinity" (Story of a Soul,* 199).

REFLECTION

Jesus tells the Israelites, "If God were your Father you would love me, for I came from God." St. Thérèse identifies her love for Jesus as the Divine Word and the Adored Eagle. St. Thérèse saw herself as a bird, weak and little. She wrote, "I look upon myself as a weak little bird, with only a light down as a covering. I am not an eagle, but I have only an eagle's EYES AND HEART" (*Story of a Soul*, 198). Her desire is to soar high "toward the divine furnace of the Holy Trinity." She aspires to intimate union with God which she knows is the outcome of prayer and virtue. She sees herself as distracted in her pursuit of Love but she is not sad, for God looks after the sinner. Her hope rests in God's unconditional love for her.

St. Thérèse encourages us to put our hope for fulfillment in the love of Jesus for us. Through grace, we try to prepare a pure heart for God, even though often enough we are caught up in trivialities. Yet, our heart sings a song of dedication. We do seek the Lord in humility and truth. That is being faithful to our destiny. And Jesus, who gave his life for us, will be faithful in His love for us.

PRAYER

Let us pray.

O God, we rely on the strength of your love for us. Inspire our hearts to seek You above all, to be faithful in following you and to spurn whatever keeps us from loving You. We make our prayer through Christ our Lord. Amen.

GOSPEL

JESUS SAID TO THE JEWS:

"Amen, amen, I say to you, whoever keeps my word will never see death." So the Jews said to him, "Now we are sure that you are possessed. Abraham died, as did the prophets, yet you say, 'Whoever keeps my word will never taste death.' Are you greater than our father Abraham, who died? Or the prophets, who died? Who do you make yourself out to be?" Jesus answered, "If I glorify myself, my glory is worth nothing; but it is my Father who glorifies me, of whom you say, 'He is our God.' You do not know him, but I know him. And if I should say that I do not know him, I would be like you a liar. But I do know him and I keep his word. Abraham your father rejoiced to see my day; he saw it and was glad." So the Jews said to him, "You are not yet fifty years old and you have seen Abraham?" Jesus said to them, "Amen, amen, I say to you, before Abraham came to be, I AM." So they picked up stones to throw at him; but Jesus hid and went out of the temple area.

JOHN 8: 51-59

ST. THÉRÈSE OF LISIEUX

"When the Lord commanded His people to love their neighbor as themselves [Lev 19:18] He had not as yet come upon the earth. Knowing the extent to which each one loved himself, He was not able to ask of His creatures a greater love than this for one's neighbor. But when Jesus gave His Apostles a new commandment, HIS OWN COMMANDMENT, as He calls it later on, it is no longer a question of loving one's neighbor as oneself but of loving him as He, Jesus, has loved him, and will love him to the consummation of the ages" (Story of a Soul, 220).

REFLECTION

Jesus in the Gospel speaks of his union and unity with the Father. He speaks of the mystery of his very person, "before Abraham came to be, I AM." The people did not comprehend his words and picked up stones to injure him. Jesus disappeared from their sight.

St. Thérèse adds her understanding of the love expected of us in the new covenant. We are not simply called to love of neighbor but to love the other as Jesus does, without limit or conditions.

The challenge to love as Jesus loves appears particularly difficult in a narcissistic age. The path to new life hinges on our willingness to surrender: to put our agendas, our anger, our petty jealousies, and our will to have things our way aside. We need to know that God's love creates change in us as long as we are open and surrender to his will. This kind of transformation is particularly appealing during the Lenten season.

PRAYER

Let us pray.

Lord, help me to see where I may be selfish or indifferent to others. I want to do your will and to show your love to those I meet today. We make our prayer through Christ our Lord. Amen.

GOSPEL

The Jews picked up rocks to stone Jesus. Jesus answered them, "I have shown you many good works from my Father. For which of these are you trying to stone me?" The Jews answered him, "We are not stoning you for a good work but for blasphemy. You, a man, are making yourself God." Jesus answered them, "Is it not written in your law, 'I said, "You are gods"'? If it calls them gods to whom the word of God came, and Scripture cannot be set aside, can you say that the one whom the Father has consecrated and sent into the world blasphemes because I said, 'I am the Son of God'? If I do not perform my Father's works, do not believe me; but if I perform them, even if you do not believe me, believe the works, so that you may realize and understand that the Father is in me and I am in the Father." Then they tried again to arrest him; but he escaped from their power.

He went back across the Jordan to the place where John first baptized, and there he remained. Many came to him and said, "John performed no sign, but everything John said about this man was true." And many there began to believe in him.

JOHN 10: 31-42

ST. THÉRÈSE OF LISIEUX

"We are living now in an age of inventions, and we no longer have to take the trouble of climbing stairs, for, in the homes of the rich, an elevator has replaced these very successfully. I wanted to find an elevator which would raise me to Jesus, for I am too small to climb the rough stairway of perfection. I searched, then, in Scripture for some sign of this elevator, the object of my desires, and I read these words coming from the mouth of Eternal Wisdom: 'Whoever is a LITTLE ONE, let him come to me' [Prov 9:4]. And so I succeeded. I had found what I was looking for" (Story of a Soul, 207–8).

REFLECTION

Jesus states his relationship to the Father in today's reading . . . Jesus and the Father are one. St. Thérèse reveals that she seeks union with God but she believes she is too small to negotiate the stairway of perfection. As always, she seeks an answer to her dilemma, her search for an elevator, by consulting Scripture. She found that whoever is little let him or her come to me. God accepts the weak and the small. Self-images are not central to union with God. God's grace moves believers to live in faith, hope and love. These are the virtues that keep us focused upon our true destiny.

While the spiritual life should not be a constant test of our endurance, it will require a spiritual discipline. That discipline will include a commitment to regular prayer, manifest a turning away from sin to the life of the virtues and to charity in particular. Any process of purification involves some suffering but the peace and joy that accompany the development of new life are gifts that one would not want to lose ever again.

PRAYER

Let us pray.

Gracious God, I seek to turn to you for guidance and assistance all the days of my life. Too often I have only occasionally attended to your presence. I want to close any distance between us through a love for your word in Scripture and through a sacramental life. We make our prayer through Christ our Lord. Amen.

GOSPEL

Many of the Jews who had come to Mary and seen what Jesus had done began to believe in him. But some of them went to the Pharisees and told them what Jesus had done. So the chief priests and the Pharisees convened the Sanhedrin and said, "What are we going to do? This man is performing many signs. If we leave him alone, all will believe in him, and the Romans will come and take away both our land and our nation." But one of them, Caiaphas, who was high priest that year, said to them "You know nothing, nor do you consider that it is better for you that one man should die instead of the people, so that the whole nation may not perish." He did not say this on his own, but since he was high priest for that year, he prophesied that Jesus was going to die for the nation, and not only for the nation, but also to gather into one the dispersed children of God. So from that day on they planned to kill him.

So Jesus no longer walked about in public among the Jews, but he left for the region near the desert, to a town called Ephraim, and there he remained with his disciples.

Now the Passover of the Jews was near, and many went up from the country to Jerusalem before Passover to purify themselves. They looked for Jesus and said to one another as they were in the temple area, "What do you think? That he will not come to the feast?"

JOHN 11: 45-56

ST. THÉRÈSE OF LISIEUX

"It is very consoling to think that Jesus, the Strong God, knew our weaknesses, that He trembled at the sight of the bitter chalice, this chalice that He had in the past so ardently desired to drink. . . . Monsieur l'Abbe, your lot is really beautiful since Our Lord chose it for Himself and since He first wet His lips with the cup He is offering you" (Letter from St. Thérèse to Maurice Belliere, seminarian, dated December 26, 1896 in *The Letters of St. Thérèse*, vol. 2, 1042).

REFLECTION

St. John's Gospel today tells us that "from that day on they planned to kill him." So, a decision was made and the final week of Lent will show how that decision unfolded. St. Thérèse's quotation from a letter she wrote to a seminarian named Maurice Belliere invites him to embrace suffering. He was ordained a priest in 1904, seven years after St. Thérèse's death.

Love and suffering are central in St. Thérèse's spirituality. She viewed suffering as a way of more closely identifying with Christ. She also saw suffering as a contribution to the salvation of souls. She offered her life for the conversion of sinners and for the good of priests. She tells Maurice Belliere that any suffering he must endure is a gift from the Lord.

It is difficult to grasp a positive side to suffering. The perspective of faith allows us to take on a larger view in which God's love converts our suffering into grace for the welfare of others.

PRAYER

Let us pray.

Loving God, may I have the conviction of St. Thérèse, namely, that my suffering may serve others through the work of Jesus Christ. Strengthen my faith so that I can identify with your passion and suffering. We make our prayer through Christ our Lord. Amen.

HOLY
WEEK

GOSPEL

AT THE PROCESSION WITH PALMS

When Jesus and the disciples drew near Jerusalem and came to Bethphage on the Mount of Olives, Jesus sent two disciples, saying to them, "Go into the village opposite you, and immediately you will find an ass tethered, and a colt with her. Untie them and bring them here to me. And if anyone should say anything to you, reply, 'The master has need of them.' Then he will send them at once." This happened so that what had been spoken through the prophet might be fulfilled: / *Say to daughter Zion, / "Behold, your king comes to you, / meek and riding on an ass, / and on a colt, the foal of a beast of burden."* / The disciples went and did as Jesus had ordered them. They brought the ass and the colt and laid their cloaks over them, and he sat upon them. The very large crowd spread their cloaks on the road, while others cut branches from the trees and strewed them on the road. The crowds preceding him and those following kept crying out and saying: / "Hosanna to the Son of David; / blessed is the he who comes in the name of the Lord; / hosanna in the highest." / And when he entered Jerusalem the whole city was shaken and asked, "Who is this?" And the crowds replied, "This is Jesus the prophet, from Nazareth in Galilee."

MATTHEW 21: 1-11

GOSPEL

MASS

One of the Twelve, who was called Judas Iscariot, went to the chief priests and said, "What are you willing to give me if I hand him over to you?" They paid him thirty pieces of silver, and from that time on he looked for an opportunity to hand him over.

On the first day of the Feast of Unleavened Bread, the disciples approached Jesus and said, "Where do you want us to prepare for you to eat the Passover?" He said, "Go into the city to a certain man and tell him, 'The teacher says, "My appointed time draws near; in your house I shall celebrate the Passover with my disciples."'"The disciples then did as Jesus had ordered, and prepared the Passover.

When it was evening, he reclined at table with the Twelve. And while they were eating, he said, "Amen, I say to you, one of you will betray me." Deeply distressed at this, they began to say to him one after another, "Surely it is not I, Lord?" He said in reply, "He who has dipped his hand into the dish with me is the one who will betray me. The Son of Man indeed goes, as it is written of him, but woe to that man by whom the Son of Man is betrayed. It would be better for that man if he had never been born." Then Judas, his betrayer, said in reply, "Surely it is not I, Rabbi?" He answered, "You have said so."

While they were eating, Jesus took bread, said the blessing, broke it, and giving it to his disciples said, "Take and eat; this is my body." Then he took a cup, gave thanks, and gave it to them, saying, "Drink from it, all of you, for this is my blood of the covenant, which will be shed on behalf of many for the forgiveness of sins. I tell you, from now on I shall not drink this fruit of the vine until the day when I drink it with you new in the kingdom of my Father." Then, after singing a hymn, they went out to the Mount of Olives.

Then Jesus said to them, "This night all of you will have your faith in me shaken, for it is written: / *I will strike the shepherd,* / *and the sheep of the flock will be dispersed;* / but after I have been raised up, I shall go before you to Galilee." Peter said to him in reply, "Though all may have their faith in you shaken, mine will never be." Jesus said to him, "Amen, I say to you, this very night before the cock crows, you will deny me three times." Peter said to him, "Even though I should have to die with you, I will not deny you." And all the disciples spoke likewise.

Then Jesus came with them to a place called Gethsemane, and he said to his disciples, "Sit here while I go over there and pray." He took along Peter and the two sons of Zebedee, and began to feel sorrow and distress. Then he said to them, "My soul is sorrowful even to death. Remain here and keep watch with me." He advanced a little and fell prostrate in prayer, saying, "My Father, if it is possible, let this cup pass from me; yet, not as I will, but as you will." When he returned to his disciples he found them asleep. He said to Peter, "So you could not keep watch with me for one hour? Watch and pray that you may not undergo the test. The spirit is willing, but the flesh is weak." Withdrawing a second time, he prayed again, "My Father, if it is not possible that this cup pass without my drinking it, your will be done!" Then he returned once more and found them asleep, for they could not keep their eyes open. He left them and withdrew again and prayed a third time, saying the same thing again. Then he returned to his disciples and said to them, "Are you still sleeping and taking your rest? Behold, the hour is at hand when the Son of Man is to be handed over to sinners. Get up, let us go. Look, my betrayer is at hand."

While he was still speaking, Judas, one of the Twelve, arrived, accompanied by a large crowd, with swords and clubs, who had come from the chief priests and the elders of the people. His betrayer had arranged a sign with them, saying, "The man I shall kiss is the one; arrest him." Immediately he went over to Jesus and said, "Hail, Rabbi!" and he kissed him. Jesus answered him, "Friend, do what you have come for." Then stepping forward they laid hands on Jesus and arrested him. And behold, one of those who accompanied Jesus put his hand to his sword, drew it, and struck the high priest's servant, cutting off his ear. Then Jesus said to him, "Put your sword back into its sheath, for all who take the sword will perish by the sword. Do you think that I cannot call upon my Father and he will not provide me at this moment with more than twelve legions of angels? But then how would the Scriptures be fulfilled which say that it must come to pass in this way?" At that hour Jesus said to the crowds, "Have you come out as against a robber, with swords and clubs to seize me? Day after day I sat teaching in the temple area, yet you did not arrest me. But all this has come to pass that the writings of the prophets may be fulfilled." Then all the disciples left him and fled.

Those who had arrested Jesus led him away to Caiaphas the high priest, where the scribes and the elders were assembled. Peter was following him at a distance as far as the high priest's courtyard, and going inside he sat down with the servants to see the outcome. The chief priests and the entire Sanhedrin kept trying to obtain false testimony against Jesus in order to put him to death, but they found none, though many false witnesses came forward. Finally two came forward who stated, "This man said, 'I can destroy the temple of God and within three days rebuild it.'" The high priest rose and addressed him, "Have you no answer? What are these men testifying against you?" But Jesus was silent. Then the high priest said to him, "I order you to tell us under oath before the living God whether you are the Christ, the Son of God." Jesus said to him in reply, "You have said so. But I tell you: / From now on you will see 'the Son of Man / seated at the right hand of the Power' / and 'coming on the clouds of heaven.'" / Then the high priest tore his robes and said, "He has blasphemed! What further need have we of witnesses? You have now heard the blasphemy; what is your opinion?" They said in reply, "He deserves to die!" Then they spat in his face and struck him, while some slapped him, saying, "Prophesy for us, Christ: who is it that struck you?"

Now Peter was sitting outside in the courtyard. One of the maids came over to him and said, "You too were with Jesus the Galilean." But he denied it in front of everyone, saying, "I do not know what you are talking about!" As he went out to the gate, another girl saw him and said to those who were there, "This man was with Jesus the Nazorean." Again he denied it with an oath, "I do not know the man!" A little later the bystanders came over and said to Peter, "Surely you too are one of them; even your speech gives you away." At that he began to curse and to swear, "I do not know the man." And immediately a cock crowed. Then Peter remembered the word that Jesus had spoken: "Before the cock crows you will deny me three times." He went out and began to weep bitterly.

When it was morning, all the chief priests and the elders of the people took counsel against Jesus to put him to death. They bound him, led him away, and handed him over to Pilate, the governor.

Then Judas, his betrayer, seeing that Jesus had been condemned, deeply regretted what he had done. He returned the thirty pieces of silver to the chief priests and elders, saying, "I have sinned in betraying innocent blood." They said, "What is that to us? Look to it yourself." Flinging the money into the temple, he departed and went off and hanged himself. The chief priests gathered up the money, but said, "It is not lawful to deposit this in the temple treasury, for it is the price of blood." After consultation, they used it to buy the potter's field as a burial place for foreigners. That is why that field even today is called the Field of Blood. Then was fulfilled what had been said through Jeremiah the prophet, / *And they took the thirty pieces of silver,* / *the value of a man with a price on his head,* / *a price set by some of the Israelites,* / *and they paid it out for the potter's field* / *just as the Lord had commanded me.*

Now Jesus stood before the governor, who questioned him, "Are you the king of the Jews?" Jesus said, "You say so." And when he was accused by the chief priests and elders, he made no answer. Then Pilate said to him, "Do you not hear how many things they are testifying against you?" But he did not answer him one word, so that the governor was greatly amazed.

Now on the occasion of the feast the governor was accustomed to release to the crowd one prisoner whom they wished. And at that time they had a notorious prisoner called Barabbas. So when they had assembled, Pilate said to them, "Which one do you want me to release to you, Barabbas, or Jesus called Christ?" For he knew that it was out of envy that they had handed him over. While he was still seated on the bench, his wife sent him a message, "Have nothing to do with that righteous man. I suffered much in a dream today because of him." The chief priests and the elders persuaded the crowds to ask for Barabbas but to destroy Jesus. The governor said to them in reply, "Which of the two do you want me to release to you?" They answered, "Barabbas!" Pilate said to them, "Then what shall I do with Jesus called Christ?" They all said, "Let him be crucified!" But he said, "Why? What evil has he done?" They only shouted the louder, "Let him be crucified!" When Pilate saw that he was not succeeding at all, but that a riot was breaking out instead, he took water and washed his hands in the sight of the crowd, saying, "I am innocent of this man's blood. Look to it yourselves." And the whole people said in reply, "His blood be upon us and upon our children." Then he released Barabbas to them, but after he had Jesus scourged, he handed him over to be crucified.

Then the soldiers of the governor took Jesus inside the praetorium and gathered the whole cohort around him. They stripped off his clothes and threw a scarlet military cloak about him. Weaving a crown out of thorns, they placed it on his head, and a reed in his right hand. And kneeling before him, they mocked him, saying, "Hail, King of the Jews!" They spat upon him and took the reed and kept striking him on the head. And when they had mocked him, they stripped him of the cloak, dressed him in his own clothes, and led him off to crucify him.

As they were going out, they met a Cyrenian named Simon; this man they pressed into service to carry his cross.

And when they came to a place called Golgotha — which means Place of the Skull —, they gave Jesus wine to drink mixed with gall. But when he had tasted it, he refused to drink. After they had crucified him, they divided his garments by casting lots; then they sat down and kept watch over him there. And they placed over his head the written charge against him: This is Jesus, the King of the Jews. Two revolutionaries were crucified with him, one on his right and the other on his left. Those passing by reviled him, shaking their heads and saying, "You who would destroy the temple and rebuild it in three days, save yourself, if you are the Son of God, and come down from the cross!" Likewise the chief priests with the scribes and elders mocked him and said, "He saved others; he cannot save himself. So he is the king of Israel! Let him come down from the cross now, and we will believe in him. He trusted in God; let him deliver him now if he wants him. For he said, 'I am the Son of God.'" The revolutionaries who were crucified with him also kept abusing him in the same way.

From noon onward, darkness came over the whole land until three in the afternoon. And about three o'clock Jesus cried out in a loud voice, *"Eli, Eli, lema sabachthani?"* which means, "My God, my God, why have you forsaken me?" Some of the bystanders who heard it said, "This one is calling for Elijah." Immediately one of them ran to get a sponge; he soaked it in wine, and putting it on a reed, gave it to him to drink. But the rest said, "Wait, let us see if Elijah comes to save him." But Jesus cried out again in a loud voice, and gave up his spirit.

Here all kneel and pause for a short time.

And behold, the veil of the sanctuary was torn in two from top to bottom. The earth quaked, rocks were split, tombs were opened, and the bodies of many saints who had fallen asleep were raised. And coming forth from their tombs after his resurrection, they entered the holy city and appeared to many. The centurion and the men with him who were keeping watch over Jesus feared greatly when they saw the earthquake and all that was happening, and they said, "Truly, this was the Son of God!" There were many women there, looking on from a distance, who had followed Jesus from Galilee, ministering to him. Among them were Mary Magdalene and Mary the mother of James and Joseph, and the mother of the sons of Zebedee.

When it was evening, there came a rich man from Arimathea named Joseph, who was himself a disciple of Jesus. He went to Pilate and asked for the body of Jesus; then Pilate ordered it to be handed over. Taking the body, Joseph wrapped it in clean linen and laid it in his new tomb that he had hewn in the rock. Then he rolled a huge stone across the entrance to the tomb and departed. But Mary Magdalene and the other Mary remained sitting there, facing the tomb.

The next day, the one following the day of preparation, the chief priests and the Pharisees gathered before Pilate and said, "Sir, we remember that this impostor while still alive said, 'After three days I will be raised up.' Give orders, then, that the grave be secured until the third day, lest his disciples come and steal him and say to the people, 'He has been raised from the dead.' This last imposture would be worse than the first." Pilate said to them, "The guard is yours; go, secure it as best you can." So they went and secured the tomb by fixing a seal to the stone and setting the guard.

MATTHEW 26: 14-75 & 27: 1-66

Shorter form: MATTHEW 27:11-54

ST. THÉRÈSE OF LISIEUX

"You know, O my God, I have never desired anything but to love *You, and I am ambitious for no other glory. Your Love has gone before me, and it has grown with me, and now it is an abyss whose depths I cannot fathom. Love attracts love, and, my Jesus, my love leaps toward Yours; it would like to fill the abyss which attracts it, but alas! it is not even like a drop of dew lost in the ocean!" (Story of a Soul,* 256*).*

REFLECTION

The Gospel of Matthew tells the story of the Passion and Death of Jesus Christ. Jesus accepted the will of the Father and his mission to save humanity from death. Yet, the price was his life.

St. Thérèse was well aware that Jesus' Passion was endured out of love for sinful humanity. She desired more than anything in life to connect to Jesus' love. She would do so by refusing Him nothing, as she said. She was convinced that Love attracts love and her life was a marvelous example of that attraction. As she once wrote: "Oh! How sweet is the way of Love! How I want to apply myself to doing the will of God always with the greatest self-surrender!" (*Story of a Soul*, 181). She wanted to pattern her life on that of Jesus.

Perhaps it is difficult for us to imagine such an engaging form of love for God as expressed in the life of St. Thérèse. How can we experience such attraction and self-surrender? Attraction and self-surrender are the work of grace within us, but we can help to prepare the soil by becoming familiar with Jesus in the four Gospels, by taking a bit of time each day to commune with God who is with us, by accepting the task of purifying our lives of deliberate sin and selfishness and by cultivating a virtuous life. The process of loving God is gradual but God always rewards fidelity to His will. In the end faith in God's love for us as well as our trust in His desire for our friendship are critical to a spiritual life.

PRAYER

Let us pray.

Lord Jesus, I want to center my whole life in a faithful relationship to you. Enable me to seek you in the ordinary and the everyday. Help me to discover your will for me each day. We make our prayer through Christ our Lord. Amen.

GOSPEL

PROCESSION WITH PALMS

When Jesus and his disciples drew near to Jerusalem, to Bethpage and Bethany at the Mount of Olives, he sent two of his disciples and said to them, "Go into the village opposite you, and immediately on entering it, you will find a colt tethered on which no one has ever sat. Untie it and bring it here. If anyone should say to you, 'Why are you doing this?' reply, 'The Master has need of it and will send it back here at once.'" So they went off and found a colt tethered at a gate outside on the street, and they untied it. Some of the bystanders said to them, "What are you doing, untying the colt?" They answered them just as Jesus had told them to, and they permitted them to do it. So they brought the colt to Jesus and put their cloaks over it. And he sat on it. Many people spread their cloaks on the road, and others spread leafy branches that they had cut from the fields. Those preceding him as well as those following kept crying out: / "Hosanna! / Blessed is he who comes in the name of the Lord! / Blessed is the kingdom of our father David that is to come! / Hosanna in the highest!"

MARK 11: 1-10

Alternative: JOHN 12:12-16

GOSPEL

MASS

The Passover and the Feast of Unleavened Bread were to take place in two days' time. So the chief priests and the scribes were seeking a way to arrest him by treachery and put him to death. They said, "Not during the festival, for fear that there may be a riot among the people."

When he was in Bethany reclining at table in the house of Simon the leper, a woman came with an alabaster jar of perfumed oil, costly genuine spikenard. She broke the alabaster jar and poured it on his head. There were some who were indignant. "Why has there been this waste of perfumed oil? It could have been sold for more than three hundred days' wages and the money given to the poor." They were infuriated with her. Jesus said, "Let her alone. Why do you make trouble for her? She has done a good thing for me. The poor you will always have with you, and whenever you wish you can do good to them, but you will not always have me. She has done what she could. She has anticipated anointing my body for burial. Amen, I say to you, wherever the gospel is proclaimed to the whole world, what she has done will be told in memory of her."

Then Judas Iscariot, one of the Twelve, went off to the chief priests to hand him over to them. When they heard him they were pleased and promised to pay him money. Then he looked for an opportunity to hand him over.

On the first day of the Feast of Unleavened Bread, when they sacrificed the Passover lamb, his disciples said to him, "Where do you want us to go and prepare for you to eat the Passover?" He sent two of his disciples and said to them, "Go into a city and a man will meet you, carrying a jar of water. Follow him. Wherever he enters, say to the master of the house, 'The Teacher says, "Where is my guest room where I may eat the Passover with my disciples?"'" Then he will show you a large upper room furnished and ready. Make the preparations for us there." The disciples then went off, entered the city, and found it just as he had told them; and they prepared the Passover.

When it was evening, he came with the Twelve. And as they reclined at table and were eating, Jesus said, "Amen, I say to you, one of you will betray me, one who is eating with me." They began to be distressed and to say to him, one by one, "Surely it is not I?" He said to them, "One of the Twelve, the one who dips with me into the dish. For the Son of Man indeed goes, as it is written of him, but woe to that man by whom the Son of Man is betrayed. It would be better for that man if he had never been born."

While they were eating, he took bread, said the blessing, broke it, and gave it to them, and said, "Take it; this is my body." Then he took a cup, gave thanks, and gave it to them, and they all drank from it. He said to them, "This is my blood of the covenant, which will be shed for many. Amen, I say to you, I shall not drink again the fruit of the vine until the day when I drink it new in the kingdom of God." Then, after singing a hymn, they went out to the Mount of Olives.

Then Jesus said to them, "All of you will have your faith shaken, for it is written: / *I will strike the shepherd, / and the sheep will be dispersed.* / But after I have been raised up, I shall go before you to Galilee." Peter said to him, "Even though all should have their faith shaken, mine will not be." Then Jesus said to him, "Amen, I say to you, this very night before the cock crows twice you will deny me three times." But he vehemently replied, "Even though I should have to die with you, I will not deny you." And they all spoke similarly.

Then they came to a place named Gethsemane, and he said to his disciples, "Sit here while I pray." He took with him Peter, James and John, and began to be troubled and distressed. Then he said to them, "My soul is sorrowful even to death. Remain here and keep watch." He advanced a little and fell to the ground and prayed that if it were possible the hour might pass by him; he said, "Abba, Father, all things are possible to you. Take this cup away from me, but not what I will but what you will." When he returned he found them asleep. He said to Peter, "Simon, are you asleep? Could you not keep watch for one hour? Watch and pray that you may not undergo the test. The spirit is willing but the flesh is weak." Withdrawing again, he prayed, saying the same thing. Then he returned once more and found them asleep, for they could not keep their eyes open and did not know what to answer him. He returned a third time and said to them, "Are you still sleeping and taking your rest? It is enough. The hour has come. Behold, the Son of Man is to be handed over to sinners. Get up, let us go. See, my betrayer is at hand."

Then, while he was still speaking, Judas, one of the Twelve, arrived, accompanied by a crowd with swords and clubs who had come from the chief priests, the scribes, and the elders. His betrayer had arranged a signal with them, saying, "The man I shall kiss is the one; arrest him and lead him away securely." He came and immediately went over to him and said, "Rabbi." And he kissed him. At this they laid hands on him and arrested him. One of the bystanders drew his sword, struck the high priest's servant, and cut off his ear. Jesus said to them in reply, "Have you come out as against a robber, with swords and clubs, to seize me? Day after day I was with you teaching in the temple area, yet you did not arrest me; but that the Scriptures may be fulfilled." And they all left him and fled. Now a young man followed him wearing nothing but a linen cloth about his body. They seized him, but he left the cloth behind and ran off naked.

They led Jesus away to the high priest, and all the chief priests and the elders and the scribes came together. Peter followed him at a distance into the high priest's courtyard and was seated with the guards, warming himself at the fire. The chief priests and the entire Sanhedrin kept trying to obtain testimony against Jesus in order to put him to death, but they found none. Many gave false witness against him, but their testimony did not agree. Some took the stand and testified falsely against him, alleging, "We heard him say, 'I will destroy this temple made with hands and within three days I will build another not made with hands.'" Even so their testimony did not agree. The high priest rose before the assembly and questioned Jesus, saying, "Have you no answer? What are these men testifying against you?" But he was silent and answered nothing. Again the high priest asked him and said to him, "Are you the Christ, the son of the Blessed One?" Then Jesus answered, "I am; / and *you will see the Son of Man / seated at the right hand of the Power / and coming with the clouds of heaven.*" / At that the high priest tore his garments and said, "What further need have we of witnesses? You have heard the blasphemy. What do you think?" They all condemned him as deserving to die. Some began to spit on him. They blindfolded him and struck him and said to him, "Prophesy!" And the guards greeted him with blows.

While Peter was below in the courtyard, one of the high priest's maids came along. Seeing Peter warming himself, she looked intently at him and said, "You too were with the Nazarene, Jesus." But he denied it saying, "I neither know nor understand what you are talking about." So he went out into the outer court. Then the cock crowed. The maid saw him and began again to say to the bystanders, "This man is one of them." Once again he denied it. A little later the bystanders said to Peter once more, "Surely you are one of them; for you too are a Galilean." He began to curse and to swear, "I do not know this man about whom you are talking." And immediately a cock crowed a second time. Then Peter remembered the word that Jesus had said to him, "Before the cock crows twice you will deny me three times." He broke down and wept.

As soon as morning came, the chief priests with the elders and the scribes, that is, the whole Sanhedrin held a council. They bound Jesus, led him away, and handed him over to Pilate. Pilate questioned him, "Are you the king of the Jews?" He said to him in reply, "You say so." The chief priests accused him of many things. Again Pilate questioned him, "Have you no answer? See how many things they accuse you of." Jesus gave him no further answer, so that Pilate was amazed.

Now on the occasion of the feast he used to release to them one prisoner whom they requested. A man called Barabbas was then in prison along with the rebels who had committed murder in a rebellion. The crowd came forward and began to ask him to do for them as he was accustomed. Pilate answered, "Do you want me to release to you the king of the Jews?" For he knew that it was out of envy that the chief priests had handed him over. But the chief priests stirred up the crowd to have him release Barabbas for them instead. Pilate again said to them in reply, "Then what do you want me to do with the man you call the king of the Jews?" They shouted again, "Crucify him." Pilate said to them, "Why? What evil has he done?" They only shouted the louder, "Crucify him." So Pilate, wishing to satisfy the crowd, released Barabbas to them and, after he had Jesus scourged, handed him over to be crucified.

The soldiers led him away inside the palace, that is, the praetorium, and assembled the whole cohort. They clothed him in purple and, weaving a crown of thorns, placed it on him. They began to salute him with, "Hail, King of the Jews!" and kept striking his head with a reed and spitting upon him. They knelt before him in homage. And when they had mocked him, they stripped him of the purple cloak, dressed him in his own clothes, and led him out to crucify him.

They pressed into service a passer-by, Simon, a Cyrenian, who was coming in from the country, the father of Alexander and Rufus, to carry his cross. They brought him to the place of Golgotha—which is translated Place of the Skull—. They gave him wine drugged with myrrh, but he did not take it. Then they crucified him and divided his garments by casting lots for them to see what each should take. It was nine o'clock in the morning when they crucified him. The inscription of the charge against him read, "The King of the Jews." With him they crucified two revolutionaries, one on his right and one on his left. Those passing by reviled him, shaking their heads and saying, "Aha! You who would destroy the temple and rebuild it in three days, save yourself by coming down from the cross." Likewise the chief priests, with the scribes, mocked him among themselves and said, "He saved others; he cannot save himself. Let the Christ, the King of Israel, come down now from the cross that we may see and believe." Those who were crucified with him also kept abusing him. At noon darkness came over the whole land until three in the afternoon. And at three o'clock Jesus cried out in a loud voice, *"Eloi, Eloi, lema sabachthani?"* which is translated, "My God, my God, why have you forsaken me?" Some of the bystanders who heard it said, "Look, he is calling Elijah." One of them ran, soaked a sponge with wine, put it on a reed and gave it to him to drink saying, "Wait, let us see if Elijah comes to take him down." Jesus gave a loud cry and breathed his last.

Here all kneel and pause for a short time.

The veil of the sanctuary was torn in two from top to bottom. When the centurion who stood facing him saw how he breathed his last he said, "Truly this man was the Son of God!"

There were also women looking on from a distance. Among them were Mary Magdalene, Mary the mother of the younger James and of Joses, and Salome. These women had followed him when he was in Galilee and ministered to him. There were also many other women who had come up with him to Jerusalem.

When it was already evening, since it was the day of preparation, the day before the sabbath, Joseph of Arimathea, a distinguished member of the council, who was himself awaiting the kingdom of God, came and courageously went to Pilate and asked for the body of Jesus. Pilate was amazed that he was already dead. He summoned the centurion and asked him if Jesus had already died. And when he learned of it from the centurion, he gave the body to Joseph. Having bought a linen cloth, he took him down, wrapped him in the linen cloth, and laid him in a tomb that had been hewn out of the rock. Then he rolled a stone against the entrance to the tomb. Mary Magdalene and Mary the mother of Joses watched where he was laid.

MARK 14: 1-72 & 15: 1-47

Shorter form: MARK 15:1-39

ST. THÉRÈSE OF LISIEUX

"When I speak of imperfect souls, I don't want to speak of spiritual imperfections since the most holy souls will be perfect only in heaven; but I want to speak of a lack of judgment, good manners, touchiness in certain characters; all these things don't make life very agreeable. I know very well that these moral infirmities are chronic, that there is no hope of a cure, but I also know that my Mother would not cease to take care of me, to try to console me, if I remained sick all my life. This is the conclusion I draw from this: I must seek out in recreation, on free days, the company of Sisters who are the least agreeable to me in order to carry out with regard to these wounded souls the office of the good Samaritan. A word, an amiable smile, often suffice to make a sad soul bloom" (Story of a Soul, 246).

In the above quotation, St. Thérèse is revealing the practical dimension of the "little way": we do not have to do grandiose gestures toward our neighbor. Rather our little signs of care and concern suffice often to bring about a deeper self-acceptance in the other.

REFLECTION

While the Passion of Jesus involved a total self-emptying, "Abba, Father, all things are possible to you. Take this cup away from me, but not what I will but what you will," he maintained always a focus upon the will of the Father. Jesus reveals a mature and committed life.

St. Thérèse shows us that the trials of everyday life are also evident within a Carmelite cloister. There are those who are moody and those who lack common sense or good manners. St. Thérèse acknowledges the world of moral infirmities by admitting that the condition is chronic. There is no hope for a cure. And she tells us how she will live in such a climate. She will be a good Samaritan.

We recognize limits in our own world of relationships. There are people we know who are quick to judge others, or are prone to anger or lacking in responsibility. We are faced with the same issue as St. Thérèse: how will we deal with the trials in our lives that seem to be with us each day? The Gospel answer calls us to love even in suffering.

PRAYER

Let us pray.

Gracious and loving God, we need your grace and help in meeting the trials that come our way so often. May we not only endure but bring to life your love and forgiveness. We ask this through Christ our Lord. Amen.

GOSPEL

PROCESSION WITH PALMS

Jesus proceeded on his journey up to Jerusalem. As he drew near to Bethpage and Bethany at the place called the Mount of Olives, he sent two of his disciples. He said, "Go into the village opposite you, and as you enter it you will find a colt tethered on which no one has ever sat. Untie it and bring it here. And if anyone should ask you, 'Why are you untying it?' you will answer, 'The Master has need of it.'" So those who had been sent went off and found everything just as he had told them. And as they were untying the colt, its owner said to them, "Why are you untying this colt?" They answered, "The Master has need of it." So they brought it to Jesus, threw their cloaks over the colt, and helped Jesus to mount. As he rode along, the people were spreading their cloaks on the road; and now as he was approaching the slope of the Mount of Olives, the whole multitude of his disciples began to praise God aloud with joy for all the mighty deeds they had seen. They proclaimed: / "Blessed is the king who comes in the name of the Lord. / Peace in heaven and glory in the highest." / Some of the Pharisees in the crowd said to him, "Teacher, rebuke your disciples." He said in reply, "I tell you, if they keep silent, the stones will cry out!"

LUKE 19: 28-40

GOSPEL

MASS

When the hour came, Jesus took his place at table with the apostles. He said to them, "I have eagerly desired to eat this Passover with you before I suffer, for, I tell you, I shall not eat it again until there is fulfillment in the kingdom of God." Then he took a cup, gave thanks, and said, "Take this and share it among yourselves; for I tell you that from this time on I shall not drink of the fruit of the vine until the kingdom of God comes." Then he took the bread, said the blessing, broke it, and gave it to them, saying, "This is my body, which will be given for you; do this in memory of me." And likewise the cup after they had eaten, saying, "This cup is the new covenant in my blood, which will be shed for you.

"And yet behold, the hand of the one who is to betray me is with me on the table; for the Son of Man indeed goes as it has been determined; but woe to that man by whom he is betrayed." And they began to debate among themselves who among them would do such a deed.

Then an argument broke out among them about which of them should be regarded as the greatest. He said to them, "The kings of the Gentiles lord it over them and those in authority over them are addressed as 'Benefactors'; but among you it shall not be so. Rather, let the greatest among you be as the youngest, and the leader as the servant. For who is greater: the one seated at table or the one who serves? Is it not the one seated at table? I am among you as the one who serves. It is you who have stood by me in my trials; and I confer a kingdom on you, just as my Father has conferred one on me, that you may eat and drink at my table in my kingdom; and you will sit on thrones judging the twelve tribes of Israel.

"Simon, Simon, behold Satan has demanded to sift all of you like wheat, but I have prayed that your own faith may not fail; and once you have turned back, you must strengthen your brothers." He said to him, "Lord, I am prepared to go to prison and to die with you." But he replied, "I tell you, Peter, before the cock crows this day, you will deny three times that you know me."

He said to them, "When I sent you forth without a money bag or a sack or sandals, were you in need of anything?" "No, nothing," they replied. He said to them, "But now one who has a money bag should take it, and likewise a sack, and one who does not have a sword should sell his cloak and buy one. For I tell you that this Scripture must be fulfilled in me, namely, *He was counted among the wicked;* and indeed what is written about me is coming to fulfillment." Then they said, "Lord, look, there are two swords here." But he replied, "It is enough!"

Then going out, he went, as was his custom, to the Mount of Olives, and the disciples followed him. When he arrived at the place he said to them, "Pray that you may not undergo the test." After withdrawing about a stone's throw from them and kneeling, he prayed, saying, "Father, if you are willing, take this cup away from me; still, not my will but yours be done." And to strengthen him an angel from heaven appeared to him. He was in such agony and he prayed so fervently that his sweat became like drops of blood falling on the ground. When he rose from prayer and returned to his disciples, he found them sleeping from grief. He said to them, "Why are you sleeping? Get up and pray that you may not undergo the test."

While he was still speaking, a crowd approached and in front was one of the Twelve, a man named Judas. He went up to Jesus to kiss him. Jesus said to him, "Judas, are you betraying the Son of Man with a kiss?" His disciples realized what was about to happen, and they asked, "Lord, shall we strike with a sword?" And one of them struck the high priest's servant and cut off his right ear. But Jesus said in reply, "Stop, no more of this!" Then he touched the servant's ear and healed him. And Jesus said to the chief priests and temple guards and elders who had come for him, "Have you come out as against a robber, with swords and clubs? Day after day I was with you in the temple area, and you did not seize me; but this is your hour, the time for the power of darkness."

After arresting him they led him away and took him into the house of the high priest; Peter was following at a distance. They lit a fire in the middle of the courtyard and sat around it, and Peter sat down with them. When a maid saw him seated in the light, she looked intently at him and said, "This man too was with him." But he denied it saying, "Woman, I do not know him." A short while later someone else saw him and said, "You too are one of them"; but Peter answered, "My friend, I am not." About an hour later, still another insisted, "Assuredly, this man too was with him, for he also is a Galilean." But Peter said, "My friend, I do not know what you are talking about." Just as he was saying this, the cock crowed, and the Lord turned and looked at Peter; and Peter remembered the word of the Lord, how he had said to him, "Before the cock crows today, you will deny me three times." He went out and began to weep bitterly. The men who held Jesus in custody were ridiculing and beating him. They blindfolded him and questioned him, saying, "Prophesy! Who is it that struck you?" And they reviled him in saying many other things against him.

When day came the council of elders of the people met, both chief priests and scribes, and they brought him before their Sanhedrin. They said, "If you are the Christ, tell us," but he replied to them, "If I tell you, you will not believe, and if I question, you will not respond. But from this time on the Son of Man will be seated at the right hand of the power of God." They all asked, "Are you then the Son of God?" He replied to them, "You say that I am." Then they said, "What further need have we for testimony? We have heard it from his own mouth."

Then the whole assembly of them arose and brought him before Pilate. They brought charges against him, saying, "We found this man misleading our people; he opposes the payment of taxes to Caesar and maintains that he is the Christ, a king." Pilate asked him, "Are you the king of the Jews?" He said to him in reply, "You say so." Pilate then addressed the chief priests and the crowds, "I find this man not guilty." But they were adamant and said, "He is inciting the people with his teaching throughout all Judea, from Galilee where he began even to here."

On hearing this Pilate asked if the man was a Galilean; and upon learning that he was under Herod's jurisdiction, he sent him to Herod, who was in Jerusalem at that time. Herod was very glad to see Jesus; he had been wanting to see him for a long time, for he had heard about him and had been hoping to see him perform some sign. He questioned him at length, but he gave him no answer. The chief priests and scribes, meanwhile, stood by accusing him harshly. Herod and his soldiers treated him contemptuously and mocked him, and after clothing him in resplendent garb, he sent him back to Pilate. Herod and Pilate became friends that very day, even though they had been enemies formerly. Pilate then summoned the chief priests, the rulers, and the people and said to them, "You brought this man to me and accused him of inciting the people to revolt. I have conducted my investigation in your presence and have not found this man guilty of the charges you have brought against him, nor did Herod, for he sent him back to us. So no capital crime has been committed by him. Therefore I shall have him flogged and then release him."

But all together they shouted out, "Away with this man! Release Barabbas to us." —Now Barabbas had been imprisoned for a rebellion that had taken place in the city and for murder.— Again Pilate addressed them, still wishing to release Jesus, but they continued their shouting, "Crucify him! Crucify him!" Pilate addressed them a third time, "What evil has this man done? I found him guilty of no capital crime. Therefore I shall have him flogged and then release him." With loud shouts, however, they persisted in calling for his crucifixion, and their voices prevailed. The verdict of Pilate was that their demand should be granted. So he released the man who had been imprisoned for rebellion and murder, for whom they asked, and he handed Jesus over to them to deal with as they wished.

As they led him away they took hold of a certain Simon, a Cyrenian, who was coming in from the country; and after laying the cross on him, they made him carry it behind Jesus. A large crowd of people followed Jesus, including many women who mourned and lamented him.

Jesus turned to them and said, "Daughters of Jerusalem, do not weep for me; weep instead for yourselves and for your children for indeed, the days are coming when people will say, 'Blessed are the barren, the wombs that never bore and the breasts that never nursed.' At that time people will say to the mountains, 'Fall upon us!' and to the hills, 'Cover us!' for if these things are done when the wood is green, what will happen when it is dry?" Now two others, both criminals, were led away with him to be executed.

When they came to the place called the Skull, they crucified him and the criminals there, one on his right, the other on his left. Then Jesus said, "Father, forgive them, they know not what they do." They divided his garments by casting lots. The people stood by and watched; the rulers, meanwhile, sneered at him and said, "He saved others, let him save himself if he is the chosen one, the Christ of God." Even the soldiers jeered at him. As they approached to offer him wine they called out, "If you are King of the Jews, save yourself." Above him there was an inscription that read, "This is the King of the Jews."

Now one of the criminals hanging there reviled Jesus, saying, "Are you not the Christ? Save yourself and us." The other, however, rebuking him, said in reply, "Have you no fear of God, for you are subject to the same condemnation? And indeed, we have been condemned justly, for the sentence we received corresponds to our crimes, but this man has done nothing criminal." Then he said, "Jesus, remember me when you come into your kingdom." He replied to him, "Amen, I say to you, today you will be with me in Paradise."

It was now about noon and darkness came over the whole land until three in the afternoon because of an eclipse of the sun. Then the veil of the temple was torn down the middle. Jesus cried out in a loud voice, "Father, into your hands I commend my spirit"; and when he had said this he breathed his last.

Here all kneel and pause for a short time.

The centurion who witnessed what had happened glorified God and said, "This man was innocent beyond doubt." When all the people who had gathered for this spectacle saw what had happened, they returned home beating their breasts; but all his acquaintances stood at a distance, including the women who had followed him from Galilee and saw these events.

Now there was a virtuous and righteous man named Joseph, who, though he was a member of the council, had not consented to their plan of action. He came from the Jewish town of Arimathea and was awaiting the kingdom of God. He went to Pilate and asked for the body of Jesus. After he had taken the body down, he wrapped it in a linen cloth and laid him in a rock-hewn tomb in which no one had yet been buried. It was the day of preparation, and the sabbath was about to begin. The women who had come from Galilee with him followed behind, and when they had seen the tomb and the way in which his body was laid in it, they returned and prepared spices and perfumed oils. Then they rested on the sabbath according to the commandment.

LUKE 22: 14-71 & 23: 1-56

Shorter form: LUKE 23:1-49

ST. THÉRÈSE OF LISIEUX

"The little flower transplanted to Mount Carmel was to expand under the shadow of the cross. The tears and blood of Jesus was to be her dew, and her Sun was his adorable Face veiled with tears. Until my coming to Carmel, I had never fathomed the depths of the treasures hidden in the Holy Face" (Story of a Soul, 151–52).

REFLECTION

St. Thérèse saw that her life grew and matured under the shadow of the Cross. The Holy Face of Jesus enabled her to see concretely that love comes to full expression in the reality of suffering. For St. Thérèse contemplation of the Holy Face was not primarily experienced as a call to a reparative kind of spirituality, but rather an invitation to join the Lord in prayerful acceptance of her own suffering. Her suffering came in the form of physical illness and in the pain of temptations against the existence of heaven. She was lacking any consolations.

None of us is attracted to suffering, yet St. Thérèse teaches that when we draw close to Jesus we can experience even joy in suffering. This joy is not a masochistic delight in pure suffering which is ego-centered, but rather an acceptance and joy in becoming more configured to Christ. St. Thérèse viewed her whole life as embodying "love in the heart of the Church." The vocation to love emerges in the push and pull of everyday life because we can see the difference that pure love creates.

PRAYER

Gracious God, Jesus' suffering makes us mindful of how we can be misjudged or cast aside. Help us to be strong through your grace of healing and to walk a path of commitment and generosity. We make our prayer through Christ our Lord. Amen.

GOSPEL

Six days before Passover Jesus came to Bethany, where Lazarus was, whom Jesus had raised from the dead. They gave a dinner for him there, and Martha served, while Lazarus was one of those reclining at table with him. Mary took a liter of costly perfumed oil made from genuine aromatic nard and anointed the feet of Jesus and dried them with her hair; the house was filled with the fragrance of the oil. Then Judas the Iscariot, one of his disciples, and the one who would betray him, said, "Why was this oil not sold for three hundred days' wages and given to the poor?" He said this not because he cared about the poor but because he was a thief and held the money bag and used to steal the contributions. So Jesus said, "Leave her alone. Let her keep this for the day of my burial. You always have the poor with you, but you do not always have me."

The large crowd of the Jews found out that he was there and came, not only because of him, but also to see Lazarus, whom he had raised from the dead. And the chief priests plotted to kill Lazarus too, because many of the Jews were turning away and believing in Jesus because of him.

JOHN 12: 1-11

ST. THÉRÈSE OF LISIEUX

"He [Jesus] made me understand these words of the Canticle of Canticles: 'Draw me, we shall run after you in the odor of your ointments.' Oh, Jesus, it is not even necessary to say: 'When drawing me, draw the souls who I love!' This simple statement: 'Draw me' suffices; I understand, Lord, that when a soul allows herself to be captivated by the odor of your ointments, she cannot run alone, all the souls whom she loves follow in her train; this is done without constraint, without effort, it is a natural consequence of her attraction for You" (Story of a Soul, 254).

REFLECTION

What a contrast between the mindset of Judas the Iscariot and St. Thérèse of Lisieux. Judas thought the ointment mentioned in the Gospel of John should be sold and the money given to the poor. However, Judas is perhaps thinking that he could manipulate funds in his own interest. For St. Thérèse ointment symbolizes God's call to relationship with Him. Oil and anointing are closely associated with the action of the Holy Spirit. To be drawn into the ocean of God's love is to bring along all those people who are in one's life. There exists a fundamental unity between love for God and love for neighbor.

We have been anointed in Baptism and in Confirmation, perhaps in receiving the Sacrament of the Sick or in Holy Orders. Anointing is a way of trying to touch upon the work of the Holy Spirit within us. God anoints us with His love and calls each one of us to holiness of life.

PRAYER

Let us pray.

Lord, our God, may each one of us be anointed with a deep desire to be faithful in following you. May we come to see the importance of modeling your unconditional love in all of our relationships. We make this prayer through Christ our Lord. Amen.

GOSPEL

Reclining at table with his disciples, Jesus was deeply troubled and testified, "Amen, amen, I say to you, one of you will betray me." The disciples looked at one another, at a loss as to whom he meant. One of his disciples, the one whom Jesus loved, was reclining at Jesus' side. So Simon Peter nodded to him to find out whom he meant. He leaned back against Jesus' chest and said to him, "Master, who is it?" Jesus answered, "It is the one to whom I hand the morsel after I have dipped it." So he dipped the morsel and took it and handed it to Judas, son of Simon the Iscariot. After Judas took the morsel, Satan entered him. So Jesus said to him, "What you are going to do, do quickly." Now none of those reclining at table realized why he said this to him. Some thought that since Judas kept the money bag, Jesus had told him, "Buy what we need for the feast," or to give something to the poor. So Judas took the morsel and left at once. And it was night.

When he had left, Jesus said, "Now is the Son of Man glorified, and God is glorified in him. If God is glorified in him, God will also glorify him in himself, and he will glorify him at once. My children, I will be with you only a little while longer. You will look for me, and as I told the Jews, 'Where I go you cannot come,' so now I say it to you."

Simon Peter said to him, "Master, where are you going?" Jesus answered him, "Where I am going, you cannot follow me now, though you will follow later." Peter said to him, "Master, why can I not follow you now? I will lay down my life for you." Jesus answered, "Will you lay down your life for me? Amen, amen, I say to you, the cock will not crow before you deny me three times."

JOHN 13: 21-33, 36-38

ST. THÉRÈSE OF LISIEUX

"I have suffered very much since I was on earth, but, if in my childhood I suffered with sadness, it is no longer in this way that I suffer. It is with joy and peace" (Story of a Soul, 210).

REFLECTION

Judas was willing to hand Jesus over to the authorities. Judas prepared the way for the Passion and Death of Jesus. St. Thérèse on the other hand was prepared to walk with Jesus by joining Him in His Passion. It was on Holy Thursday night into Good Friday, 1896, that St. Thérèse had her first hemoptysis. She noticed in the morning she had coughed up blood during the night. To her it was a sign that she would soon be called to heaven. "I was interiorly persuaded that Jesus . . . wanted to have me hear His first call" (*Story of a Soul*, 211). Her vivid and captivating relationship to Jesus seems beyond our imagining!

How is it possible to come to such an engaging relationship to Christ? Obviously, it is more God's doing than our own. With the assistance of God's grace we can prepare the way. For St. Thérèse it meant trusting in God's love completely, living in total self-surrender to God's will as it came more clear to her. We have to let go of trying to control everything about our lives. Jesus becomes the center of one's life and that makes all the difference.

PRAYER

Let us pray.

Loving God, help me to entrust my life totally according to your will. Let everything be done in me according to your Word. We make our prayer through Christ our Lord. Amen.

GOSPEL

One of the Twelve, who was called Judas Iscariot, went to the chief priests and said, "What are you willing to give me if I hand him over to you?" They paid him thirty pieces of silver, and from that time on he looked for an opportunity to hand him over.

On the first day of the Feast of Unleavened Bread, the disciples approached Jesus and said, "Where do you want us to prepare for you to eat the Passover?" He said, "Go into the city to a certain man and tell him, 'The teacher says, My appointed time draws near; in your house I shall celebrate the Passover with my disciples.'" The disciples then did as Jesus had ordered, and prepared the Passover.

When it was evening, he reclined at table with the Twelve. And while they were eating, he said, "Amen, I say to you, one of you will betray me." Deeply distressed at this, they began to say to him one after another, "Surely it is not I, Lord?" He said in reply, "He who has dipped his hand into the dish with me is the one who will betray me. The Son of Man indeed goes, as it is written of him, but woe to that man by whom the Son of Man is betrayed. It would be better for that man if he had never been born." Then Judas, his betrayer, said in reply, "Surely it is not I, Rabbi?" He answered, "You have said so."

MATTHEW 26: 14-25

ST. THÉRÈSE OF LISIEUX

"How will this 'story of a little white flower' come to an end? Perhaps the little flower will be plucked in your youthful freshness or else transplanted to other shores. I don't know, but what I am certain about is that God's Mercy will accompany her always" (Story of a Soul, 181).

REFLECTION

The Gospel identifies clearly that Judas is the betrayer. While he had entered into relationship with Jesus as a disciple and was in charge of the money, his heart became deviant. He did not sustain his commitment to the Lord.

St. Thérèse reflects on her future. Will she die young or will she become a missionary ("transplanted to other shores")? We know her outcome. Her discipleship of Jesus remained faithful to the end. Her life was a constant testimony to her love for Jesus and for her Carmelite Sisters.

We are faced with choices in our life. Will we remain faithful in our commitment to the Lord or will we compromise discipleship through sinful choices? The outcome of fidelity is peace and inner joy. The consequence of sin is alienation and anxiety. Lord, that I may see.

PRAYER

Let us pray.

Jesus, help me to follow you faithfully. May I always be aware of the truth of my life and have the strength to root out all illusion and false pretense. We make our prayer through Christ our Lord. Amen.

PASCHAL
TRIDUUM

GOSPEL

Jesus came to Nazareth, where he had grown up, and went according to his custom into the synagogue on the sabbath day. He stood up to read and was handed a scroll of the prophet Isaiah. He unrolled the scroll and found the passage where it was written:

> *The Spirit of the Lord is upon me,*
> *because he has anointed me*
> > *to bring glad tidings to the poor.*
> *He has sent me to proclaim liberty to captives*
> > *and recovery of sight to the blind,*
> > *to let the oppressed go free,*
> *and to proclaim a year acceptable to the Lord.*

Rolling up the scroll, he handed it back to the attendant and sat down, and the eyes of all in the synagogue looked intently at him. He said to them, "Today this Scripture passage is fulfilled in your hearing."

LUKE 4: 16-21

ST. THÉRÈSE OF LISIEUX

"I applied myself to practicing little virtues, not having the capability of practicing the great. For instance, I loved to fold up the mantles forgotten by the Sisters, and to render them all sorts of little services. Love for mortification was given me and this love was all the greater because I was allowed nothing by way of satisfying it" (Story of a Soul, 159).

† The Chrism Mass is the annual Mass when the bishop blesses the oils that will be used for the sacraments throughout the year in the diocese.

REFLECTION

Jesus announces in the synagogue that He fulfills the word of Isaiah: the Spirit of the Lord has anointed Him. He is the universal Savior and He frees the oppressed. St. Thérèse tells us that she embraces a mortified life but her works are modest in scope. Yet, her "services" toward her Sisters in community reflect a love and deep respect for others. She reveals herself as a true disciple of Jesus.

We have been anointed in our baptism to witness to Jesus in our own lives. Like St. Thérèse we can provide services to others who need a word of affirmation or a listening ear or a ride to the doctor. Many are the ways in which we can express our love for God and our love for neighbor. At times we need to fight the apathy that afflicts us in order to maintain an authentic life of discipleship.

PRAYER

Let us pray.

Lord, our God, give us the grace to follow you in fidelity and truth as expressions of our baptismal anointing. May we serve others generously and in love. We make our prayer through Christ our Lord. Amen.

GOSPEL

Before the feast of Passover, Jesus knew that his hour had come to pass from this world to the Father. He loved his own in the world and he loved them to the end. The devil had already induced Judas, son of Simon the Iscariot, to hand him over. So, during supper, fully aware that the Father had put everything into his power and that he had come from God and was returning to God, he rose from supper and took off his outer garments. He took a towel and tied it around his waist. Then he poured water into a basin and began to wash the disciples' feet and dry them with the towel around his waist. He came to Simon Peter, who said to him, "Master, are you going to wash my feet?" Jesus answered and said to him, "What I am doing, you do not understand now, but you will understand later." Peter said to him, "You will never wash my feet." Jesus answered him, "Unless I wash you, you will have no inheritance with me." Simon Peter said to him, "Master, then not only my feet, but my hands and head as well." Jesus said to him, "Whoever has bathed has no need except to have his feet washed, for he is clean all over; so you are clean, but not all." For he knew who would betray him; for this reason, he said, "Not all of you are clean."

So when he had washed their feet and put his garments back on and reclined at table again, he said to them, "Do you realize what I have done for you? You call me 'teacher' and 'master,' and rightly so, for indeed I am. If I, therefore, the master and teacher, have washed your feet, you ought to wash one another's feet. I have given you a model to follow, so that as I have done for you, you should also do."

JOHN 13: 1-15

ST. THÉRÈSE OF LISIEUX

"At the Last Supper, when He knew the hearts of His disciples were burning with a more ardent love for Him who had just given Himself to them in the unspeakable mystery of His Eucharist, this sweet Savior wished to give them a new commandment. *He said to them with inexpressible tenderness: 'A new commandment I give you that you love one another: that as I have loved you, you also love one another. By this will all men know that you are my disciples,* if you have love for one another"* (John 13:24–35, *Story of a Soul,* 219).

REFLECTION

Jesus' example at the Last Supper reveals the importance of service of others. The washing of the feet provides a model of humility and love. St. Thérèse reminds us that the gift of Jesus in the Eucharist can spark "a more ardent love for Him." And genuine love for Jesus leads us to a profound attention and love for our neighbor.

The example of Jesus on Holy Thursday can be regarded as irrelevant in a harsh and narcissistic world. A culture that promotes "looking out for self" and "taking care of number one" creates an environment of alienation and hurt. Jesus spent His life in trying to overcome the power of evil, the world of violence, hatred and apathy. St. Thérèse cultivated a will to love others, even when it cost her personal sacrifice. What is at issue here is the meaning of our humanity. A question remains: Where am I in relationship to the call of Christ to love my neighbor?

PRAYER

Let us pray.

Lord, my heart is full of gratitude for the gift of the Eucharist. I ask that you fill the hearts of our priests with zeal for your Eucharistic presence and may all Christians respond to your command to love others. We ask this through Christ our Lord. Amen.

GOSPEL

Jesus went out with his disciples across the Kidron valley to where there was a garden, into which he and his disciples entered. Judas his betrayer also knew the place, because Jesus had often met there with his disciples. So Judas got a band of soldiers and guards from the chief priests and the Pharisees and went there with lanterns, torches, and weapons. Jesus, knowing everything that was going to happen to him, went out and said to them, "Whom are you looking for?" They answered him, "Jesus the Nazorean." He said to them, "I AM." Judas his betrayer was also with them. When he said to them, "I AM," they turned away and fell to the ground. So he again asked them, "Whom are you looking for?" They said, "Jesus the Nazorean." Jesus answered, "I told you that I AM. So if you are looking for me, let these men go." This was to fulfill what he had said, "I have not lost any of those you gave me." Then Simon Peter, who had a sword, drew it, struck the high priest's slave, and cut off his right ear. The slave's name was Malchus. Jesus said to Peter, "Put your sword into its scabbard. Shall I not drink the cup that the Father gave me?"

So the band of soldiers, the tribune, and the Jewish guards seized Jesus, bound him, and brought him to Annas first. He was the father-in-law of Caiaphas, who was high priest that year. It was Caiaphas who had counseled the Jews that it was better that one man should die rather than the people.

Simon Peter and another disciple followed Jesus. Now the other disciple was known to the high priest, and he entered the courtyard of the high priest with Jesus. But Peter stood at the gate outside. So the other disciple, the acquaintance of the high priest, went out and spoke to the gatekeeper and brought Peter in. Then the maid who was the gatekeeper said to Peter, "You are not one of this man's disciples, are you?" He said, "I am not." Now the slaves and the guards were standing around a charcoal fire that they had made, because it was cold, and were warming themselves. Peter was also standing there keeping warm.

The high priest questioned Jesus about his disciples and about his doctrine. Jesus answered him, "I have spoken publicly to the world. I have always taught in a synagogue or in the temple area where all the Jews gather, and in secret I have said nothing. Why ask me? Ask those who heard me what I said to them. They know what I said." When he had said this, one of the temple guards standing there struck Jesus and said, "Is this the way you answer the high priest?" Jesus answered him, "If I have spoken wrongly, testify to the wrong; but if I have spoken rightly, why do you strike me?" Then Annas sent him bound to Caiaphas the high priest.

Now Simon Peter was standing there keeping warm. And they said to him, "You are not one of his disciples, are you?" He denied it and said, "I am not." One of the slaves of the high priest, a relative of the one whose ear Peter had cut off, said, "Didn't I see you in the garden with him?" Again Peter denied it. And immediately the cock crowed.

Then they brought Jesus from Caiaphas to the praetorium. It was morning. And they themselves did not enter the praetorium, in order not to be defiled so that they could eat the Passover. So Pilate came out to them and said, "What charge do you bring against this man?" They answered and said to him, "If he were not a criminal, we would not have handed him over to you." At this, Pilate said to them, "Take him yourselves, and judge him according to your law." The Jews answered him, "We do not have the right to execute anyone," in order that the word of Jesus might be fulfilled that he said indicating the kind of death he would die.

So Pilate went back into the praetorium and summoned Jesus and said to him, "Are you the King of the Jews?" Jesus answered, "Do you say this on your own or have others told you about me?" Pilate answered, "I am not a Jew, am I? Your own nation and the chief priests handed you over to me. What have you done?" Jesus answered, "My kingdom does not belong to this world. If my kingdom did belong to this world, my attendants would be fighting to keep me from being handed over to the Jews. But as it is, my kingdom is not here." So Pilate said to him, "Then you are a king?" Jesus answered, "You say I am a king. For this I was born and for this I came into the world, to testify to the truth. Everyone who belongs to the truth listens to my voice." Pilate said to him, "What is truth?"

When he had said this, he again went out to the Jews and said to them, "I find no guilt in him. But you have a custom that I release one prisoner to you at Passover. Do you want me to release to you the King of the Jews?" They cried out again, "Not this one but Barabbas!" Now Barabbas was a revolutionary.

Then Pilate took Jesus and had him scourged. And the soldiers wove a crown out of thorns and placed it on his head, and clothed him in a purple cloak, and they came to him and said, "Hail, King of the Jews!" And they struck him repeatedly. Once more Pilate went out and said to them, "Look, I am bringing him out to you, so that you may know that I find no guilt in him." So Jesus came out, wearing the crown of thorns and the purple cloak. And he said to them, "Behold, the man!" When the chief priests and the guards saw him they cried out, "Crucify him, crucify him!" Pilate said to them, "Take him yourselves and crucify him. I find no guilt in him." The Jews answered, "We have a law, and according to that law he ought to die, because he made himself the Son of God." Now when Pilate heard this statement, he became even more afraid, and went back into the praetorium and said to Jesus, "Where are you from?" Jesus did not answer him. So Pilate said to him, "Do you not speak to me? Do you not know that I have power to release you and I have power to crucify you?" Jesus answered him, "You would have no power over me if it had not been given to you from above. For this reason the one who handed me over to you has the greater sin." Consequently, Pilate tried to release him;

but the Jews cried out, "If you release him, you are not a Friend of Caesar. Everyone who makes himself a king opposes Caesar."

When Pilate heard these words he brought Jesus out and seated him on the judge's bench in the place called Stone Pavement, in Hebrew, Gabbatha. It was preparation day for Passover, and it was about noon. And he said to the Jews, "Behold, your king!" They cried out, "Take him away, take him away! Crucify him!" Pilate said to them, "Shall I crucify your king?" The chief priests answered, "We have no king but Caesar." Then he handed him over to them to be crucified.

So they took Jesus, and, carrying the cross himself, he went out to what is called the Place of the Skull, in Hebrew, Golgotha. There they crucified him, and with him two others, one on either side, with Jesus in the middle. Pilate also had an inscription written and put on the cross. It read, "Jesus the Nazorean, the King of the Jews." Now many of the Jews read this inscription, because the place where Jesus was crucified was near the city; and it was written in Hebrew, Latin, and Greek. So the chief priests of the Jews said to Pilate, "Do not write 'The King of the Jews,' but that he said, 'I am the King of the Jews'." Pilate answered, "What I have written, I have written."

When the soldiers had crucified Jesus, they took his clothes and divided them into four shares, a share for each soldier. They also took his tunic, but the tunic was seamless, woven in one piece from the top down. So they said to one another, "Let's not tear it, but cast lots for it to see whose it will be," in order that the passage of Scripture might be fulfilled that says:

They divided my garments among them,
and for my vesture they cast lots.

This is what the soldiers did. Standing by the cross of Jesus were his mother and his mother's sister, Mary the wife of Clopas, and Mary of Magdala. When Jesus saw his mother and the disciple there whom he loved he said to his mother, "Woman, behold, your son." Then he said to the disciple, "Behold, your mother." And from that hour the disciple took her into his home.

After this, aware that everything was now finished, in order that the Scripture might be fulfilled, Jesus said, "I thirst." There was a vessel filled with common wine. So they put a sponge soaked in wine on a sprig of hyssop and put it up to his mouth. When Jesus had taken the wine, he said, "It is finished." And bowing his head, he handed over the spirit.

Here all kneel and pause for a short time.

Now since it was preparation day, in order that the bodies might not remain on the cross on the sabbath, for the sabbath day of that week was a solemn one, the Jews asked Pilate that their legs be broken and that they be taken down. So the soldiers came and broke the legs of the first and then of the other one who was crucified with Jesus. But when they came to Jesus and saw that he was already dead, they did not break his legs, but one soldier thrust his lance into his side, and immediately blood and water flowed out. An eyewitness has testified, and his testimony is true; he knows that he is speaking the truth, so that you also may come to believe. For this happened so that the Scripture passage might be fulfilled: *Not a bone of it will be broken.* And again another passage says: *They will look upon him whom they have pierced.*

After this, Joseph of Arimathea, secretly a disciple of Jesus for fear of the Jews, asked Pilate if he could remove the body of Jesus. And Pilate permitted it. So he came and took his body. Nicodemus, the one who had first come to him at night, also came bringing a mixture of myrrh and aloes weighing about one hundred pounds. They took the body of Jesus and bound it with burial cloths along with the spices, according to the Jewish burial custom. Now in the place where he had been crucified there was a garden, and in the garden a new tomb, in which no one had yet been buried. So they laid Jesus there because of the Jewish preparation day; for the tomb was close by.

JOHN 18: 1-40 & 19: 1-42

ST. THÉRÈSE OF LISIEUX

"*I listened attentively to the sermons which I understood very poorly. The first I* did understand *and which* touched me deeply *was a sermon on the Passion preached by Father Ducellier and since then I've understood all the others*" (*Story of a Soul,* 42).

REFLECTION

We contemplate the Passion of Jesus Christ in silent prayer. So often we may fail to appreciate the humble and profound mystery of God's love for us. The Passion and Death of Jesus tell us clearly that God self-emptied in order to provide us with His saving grace.

Whatever Father Ducelliere said in his sermon on the Passion of Christ, he enabled St. Thérèse to understand something of the great mystery of Christ's love for us. Her story of holiness is centered on love. She sought to love in little gestures, her Little Way she called it.

In contemplating the Passion and Death of Jesus may we come to deepen our appreciation of the mystery of God's love for each one of us and may we come to embrace a lifetime of love for God and love for neighbor whether convenient or inconvenient.

PRAYER

Let us pray.

Lord Jesus Christ, we meet you in your Passion with sorrow for our sins and filled with a desire to follow you more faithfully. Help each one of us to be grateful for your gracious love. We make our prayer through Christ our Lord. Amen.

GOSPEL

After the sabbath, as the first day of the week was dawning, Mary Magdalene and the other Mary came to see the tomb. And behold, there was a great earthquake; for an angel of the Lord descended from heaven, approached, rolled back the stone, and sat upon it. His appearance was like lightning and his clothing was white as snow. The guards were shaken with fear of him and became like dead men. Then the angel said to the women in reply, "Do not be afraid! I know that you are seeking Jesus the crucified. He is not here, for he has been raised just as he said. Come and see the place where he lay. Then go quickly and tell his disciples, 'He has been raised from the dead, and he is going before you to Galilee; there you will see him.' Behold, I have told you." Then they went away quickly from the tomb, fearful yet overjoyed, and ran to announce this to his disciples. And behold, Jesus met them on their way and greeted them. They approached, embraced his feet, and did him homage. Then Jesus said to them, "Do not be afraid. Go tell my brothers to go to Galilee, and there they will see me."

MATTHEW 28: 1-10

ST. THÉRÈSE OF LISIEUX

"I thank you, O my God! For all the graces You have granted me, especially the grace of making me pass through the crucible of suffering. It is with joy I shall contemplate You on the Last Day carrying the scepter of Your Cross. Since you deigned to give me a share in this very precious Cross, I hope in heaven to resemble You and to see shining in my glorified body the sacred stigmata of Your Passion" ("Act of Oblation to Merciful Love" in *Story of a Soul*, 277).

REFLECTION

In nineteenth-century French spirituality the Passion of Jesus seemed to attract more attention than the victory of the Resurrection. St. Thérèse was very attracted to viewing her own life in relationship to Jesus' Passion. The Passion revealed to her the profound commitment of Jesus Christ to the salvation of people. The mystery of His love became quite palpable in His Passion and Death.

In the liturgical life of the Church today we hold together in the sacred Triduum the life, death, and Resurrection of Jesus. The whole passage of Jesus is from death to life. The Christian way embraces the Paschal mystery: we pass from death to sin to the new life of integrity and the virtues through the saving grace of Jesus Christ. The binding power of the Christian way is the virtue of self-emptying love that God's grace provides.

PRAYER

Let us pray.

Jesus, help me to know you in this holy Triduum. May I contemplate your love for me and for all people so that I may become a source of your peace in the world. We make our prayer through Christ our Lord. Amen.

GOSPEL

When the sabbath was over, Mary Magdalene, Mary, the mother of James, and Salome bought spices so that they might go and anoint him. Very early when the sun had risen, on the first day of the week, they came to the tomb. They were saying to one another, "Who will roll back the stone for us from the entrance to the tomb?" When they looked up, they saw that the stone had been rolled back; it was very large. On entering the tomb they saw a young man sitting on the right side, clothed in a white robe, and they were utterly amazed. He said to them, "Do not be amazed! You seek Jesus of Nazareth, the crucified. He has been raised; he is not here. Behold the place where they laid him. "But go and tell his disciples and Peter, 'He is going before you to Galilee; there you will see him, as he told you.'"

MARK 16: 1-7

ST. THÉRÈSE OF LISIEUX

"In the morning of September 8, I felt as though I was flooded with a river of peace, and it was in this peace, and it was in this peace 'which surpasses all understanding' [Philippians 4:7] that I pronounced my Holy Vows. My union with Jesus was effected not in the midst of thunder and lightening, that is, in extraordinary graces, but in the bosom of a light breeze similar to the one our Father St. Elijah heard on the Mount" (Story of a Soul, 166–67).

REFLECTION

Obviously, the apostles and disciples of Jesus were devastated by Jesus' passion and death. More than likely they thought His story had ended and nothing more could be said, even though Jesus had indicated He would rise. The simple story of the empty tomb indicated more had happened: "He is going before you to Galilee; there you shall see Him, as He told you".

St. Thérèse tells us that her union with Jesus, affirmed by her Vows, happened in a simple way, like a light breeze. Much that occurs in the spiritual life happens in the ordinary and the routine. Our prayer can rise up to God devoid of all consolation. Our faithful commitment to Christ can encounter struggle, doubt, and timidity. Yet, deep within the human spirit, the soul, God continues to be at work in bringing about a union with Him that surpasses all understanding.

PRAYER

Let us pray.

Jesus, your Resurrection leads us to praise and to adore You, and we live with a profound sense of hope. Give us the courage to witness to the truth of your Gospel. We make our prayer through Christ our Lord. Amen.

GOSPEL

At daybreak on the first day of the week the women who had come from Galilee with Jesus took the spices they had prepared and went to the tomb. They found the stone rolled away from the tomb; but when they entered, they did not find the body of the Lord Jesus. While they were puzzling over this, behold, two men in dazzling garments appeared to them. They were terrified and bowed their faces to the ground. They said to them, "Why do you seek the living one among the dead? He is not here, but he has been raised. Remember what he said to you while he was still in Galilee, that the Son of Man must be handed over to sinners and be crucified, and rise on the third day." And they remembered his words. Then they returned from the tomb and announced all these things to the eleven and to all others. The women were Mary Magdalene, Joanna, and Mary the mother of James; the others who accompanied them also told this to the apostles, but their story seemed like nonsense and they did not believe them. But Peter got up and ran to the tomb, bent down, and saw the burial cloths alone; then he went home amazed at what had happened.

LUKE 24: 1-12

ST. THÉRÈSE OF LISIEUX

"O Jesus, my Beloved, who could express the tenderness and sweetness with which you are guiding my soul! It pleases You to cause the rays of Your grace to shine through even in the midst of the darkest storm! Jesus, the storm was raging very strongly in my soul ever since the beautiful feast of Your victory, the radiant feast of Easter" (Story of a Soul, 190).

REFLECTION

The storm raging within St. Thérèse is her struggle with doubt about the existence of heaven, a temptation that lasted even up to her death. Yet, as she suffered from the temptation she seemed to enjoy peace at a deeper level of her being. During this period, she continued to write letters, to compose poems and plays which reflect calm, joy, and a profound commitment to Jesus Christ.

The presence of doubt is not an uncommon phenomenon in Christian life. It may be a question about Christ's presence in the Eucharist or the very existence of God or a questioning of the Church as an institution. St. Thérèse's approach was to make many acts of faith to counteract the temptation to doubt. Christ's comment to his apostles is worthy of reflection: "Blessed are those who have not seen and have believed" (John 20:29).

PRAYER

Let us pray.

Lord, help us to be strong when we have to confront doubt or temptation in our lives. Our great desire is to be faithful in following you. Help us always to follow our Catholic tradition and its teachings in the midst of a fragile and uncertain world. We make our prayer through Christ our Lord. Amen.

EASTER
SUNDAY

GOSPEL

On the first day of the week, Mary of Magdala came to the tomb early in the morning, while it was still dark, and saw the stone removed from the tomb. So she ran and went to Simon Peter and to the other disciple whom Jesus loved, and told them, "They have taken the Lord from the tomb, and we don't know where they put him." So Peter and the other disciple went out and came to the tomb. They both ran, but the other disciple ran faster than Peter and arrived at the tomb first; he bent down and saw the burial cloths there, but did not go in. When Simon Peter arrived after him, he went into the tomb and saw the burial cloths there, and the cloth that had covered his head, not with the burial cloths but rolled up in a separate place. Then the other disciple also went in, the one who had arrived at the tomb first, and he saw and believed. For they did not yet understand the Scripture that he had to rise from the dead.

JOHN 20: 1-9

Alternative readings from Easter Vigil or LUKE 24:13-35 at an afternoon or evening Mass.

ST. THÉRÈSE OF LISIEUX

"You might believe I will sing Alleluia during Lent . . . Oh! No, I shall content myself with following Jesus on His painful way; I shall hang my harp on the willows on the shores of the rivers of Babylon. . . . But after the Resurrection, I shall take up my harp again, forgetting for a moment I am exiled; with you I shall sing the joy of serving Jesus and living in His house, the joy of being His spouse for time and Eternity" (Letter of Thérèse to Sister Thérèse Dosithee in *The Letters of St. Thérèse*, vol. 2, letter 175, 899).

REFLECTION

St. Thérèse registers great joy at the conclusion of the Lenten season when she will celebrate the Lord's Resurrection. Her joy arises from her role as spouse of Jesus. One can read between the lines her enthusiasm for her relationship to Christ.

We may feel that our relationship to the Lord lacks the spark that emanates from St. Thérèse. But we are not called to depend on good feelings and consolation. A solid spiritual life is rooted in faith, hope, and love. We may experience a certain dryness and even darkness in relation to the mystery of God. Such was the experience of Blessed Teresa of Calcutta and St. Thérèse. In fact, St. Thérèse made the point that her nine years in the Carmelite monastery in Lisieux was not steeped in consolations. Fidelity in prayer and a life of integrity no matter how much we may lack consolations are signs of holiness of life.

PRAYER

Let us pray.

Lord, show me the path to holiness of life. May the Paschal mystery be a grace in my life so that I may follow you in peace and joy. We make our prayer through Christ our Lord. Amen.

APPENDIX A:
CALENDAR OF LENT 2010-2019
& LECTIONARY CYCLE

Ash Wednesday–Easter

Year	Sunday Year	Lent	Date
2010	C	Ash Wednesday	February 17
		1st Sunday of Lent	February 21
		2nd Sunday of Lent	February 28
		3rd Sunday of Lent	March 7
		4th Sunday of Lent	March 14
		5th Sunday of Lent	March 21
		Palm Sunday	March 28
		Paschal Triduum	April 1
		Easter Sunday	April 4
2011	A	Ash Wednesday	March 9
		1st Sunday of Lent	March 13
		2nd Sunday of Lent	March 20
		3rd Sunday of Lent	March 27
		4th Sunday of Lent	April 3
		5th Sunday of Lent	April 10
		Palm Sunday	April 17
		Paschal Triduum	April 21
		Easter Sunday	April 24

Year	Sunday Year	Lent	Date
2012	B	Ash Wednesday	February 22
		1st Sunday of Lent	February 26
		2nd Sunday of Lent	March 4
		3rd Sunday of Lent	March 11
		4th Sunday of Lent	March 18
		5th Sunday of Lent	March 25
		Palm Sunday	April 1
		Paschal Triduum	April 5
		Easter Sunday	April 8
2013	C	Ash Wednesday	February 13
		1st Sunday of Lent	February 17
		2nd Sunday of Lent	February 24
		3rd Sunday of Lent	March 3
		4th Sunday of Lent	March 10
		5th Sunday of Lent	March 17
		Palm Sunday	March 24
		Paschal Triduum	March 28
		Easter Sunday	March 31

Year	Sunday Year	Lent	Date
2014	A	Ash Wednesday	March 5
		1st Sunday of Lent	March 9
		2nd Sunday of Lent	March 16
		3rd Sunday of Lent	March 23
		4th Sunday of Lent	March 30
		5th Sunday of Lent	April 6
		Palm Sunday	April 13
		Paschal Triduum	April 17
		Easter Sunday	April 20
2015	B	Ash Wednesday	February 18
		1st Sunday of Lent	February 22
		2nd Sunday of Lent	March 1
		3rd Sunday of Lent	March 8
		4th Sunday of Lent	March 15
		5th Sunday of Lent	March 22
		Palm Sunday	March 29
		Paschal Triduum	April 2
		Easter Sunday	April 5

Year	Sunday Year	Lent	Date
2016	C	Ash Wednesday	February 10
		1st Sunday of Lent	February 14
		2nd Sunday of Lent	February 21
		3rd Sunday of Lent	February 28
		4th Sunday of Lent	March 6
		5th Sunday of Lent	March 13
		Palm Sunday	March 20
		Paschal Triduum	March 24
		Easter Sunday	March 27
2017	A	Ash Wednesday	March 1
		1st Sunday of Lent	March 5
		2nd Sunday of Lent	March 12
		3rd Sunday of Lent	March 19
		4th Sunday of Lent	March 26
		5th Sunday of Lent	April 2
		Palm Sunday	April 9
		Paschal Triduum	April 13
		Easter Sunday	April 16

Year	Sunday Year	Lent	Date
2018	B	Ash Wednesday	February 14
		1st Sunday of Lent	February 18
		2nd Sunday of Lent	February 25
		3rd Sunday of Lent	March 4
		4th Sunday of Lent	March 11
		5th Sunday of Lent	March 18
		Palm Sunday	March 25
		Paschal Triduum	March 29
		Easter Sunday	April 1
2019	C	Ash Wednesday	March 6
		1st Sunday of Lent	March 10
		2nd Sunday of Lent	March 17
		3rd Sunday of Lent	March 24
		4th Sunday of Lent	March 31
		5th Sunday of Lent	April 7
		Palm Sunday	April 14
		Paschal Triduum	April 18
		Easter Sunday	April 21

APPENDIX B:
SELECTIONS FROM THE
WRITINGS OF ST. THÉRÈSE OF LISIEUX

Ash Wednesday	*Story of a Soul*, 14
Thursday	*Story of a Soul*, 143
Friday	*The Poetry of St. Thérèse*, 104
Saturday	*Story of a Soul*, 99
1st Sunday A	*Story of a Soul*, 219
1st Sunday B	*Story of a Soul*, 179
1st Sunday C	*Story of a Soul*, 209–10
Monday 1	*Story of a Soul*, 259
Tuesday 1	*Story of a Soul*, 243
Wednesday 1	*Story of a Soul*, 207
Thursday 1	*Story of a Soul*, 221
Friday 1	*Story of a Soul*, 222
Saturday 1	*Story of a Soul*, 225
2nd Sunday A	*The Poetry of St. Thérèse*, 102
2nd Sunday B	*Story of a Soul*, 221
2nd Sunday C	*Story of a Soul*, 27
Monday 2	*Story of a Soul*, 234
Tuesday 2	*Story of a Soul*, 250
Wednesday 2	*Story of a Soul*, 220
Thursday 2	*Story of a Soul*, 257
Friday 2	*Story of a Soul*, 181
Saturday 2	*Story of a Soul*, 101–2; Ez 16:8–13
3rd Sunday A	*Story of a Soul*, 189
3rd Sunday B	*Story of a Soul*, 104
3rd Sunday C	*Story of a Soul*, 259
Monday 3	*Story of a Soul*, 195–96
Tuesday 3	*The Letters of St. Thérèse*, 2:1093
Wednesday 3	*Story of a Soul*, 226
Thursday 3	*Story of a Soul*, 166
Friday 3	*Story of a Soul*, 221
Saturday 3	*Story of a Soul*, 181–82

4th Sunday A	*Story of a Soul*, 15
4th Sunday B	*Story of a Soul*, 157
4th Sunday C	*Story of a Soul*, 152
Monday 4	*The Letters of St. Thérèse*, 2:865
Tuesday 4	*Story of a Soul*, 84
Wednesday 4	*The Poetry of St. Thérèse*, 102
Thursday 4	*Story of a Soul*, 197
Friday 4	*The Letters of St. Thérèse*, 2:1138
Saturday 4	*Story of a Soul*, 192
5th Sunday A	*Story of a Soul*, 15
5th Sunday B	*Story of a Soul*, 218
5th Sunday C	*Story of a Soul*, 15
Monday 5 Years A and B	*Story of a Soul*, 100
Monday Year C	*Story of a Soul*, 98
Tuesday 5	*Story of a Soul*, 102
Wednesday 5	*Story of a Soul*, 199
Thursday 5	*Story of a Soul*, 220
Friday 5	*Story of a Soul*, 207–8
Saturday 5	*The Letters of St. Thérèse*, 2:1042
Passion Sunday A	*Story of a Soul*, 256
Passion Sunday B	*Story of a Soul*, 246
Passion Sunday C	*Story of a Soul*, 151–52
Monday of Holy Week	*Story of a Soul*, 254
Tuesday of Holy Week	*Story of a Soul*, 210
Wednesday of Holy Week	*Story of a Soul*, 181
Chrism Mass	*Story of a Soul*, 159
Holy Thursday	*Story of a Soul*, 219
Good Friday	*Story of a Soul*, 42
Holy Saturday-Vigil Mass A	*Story of a Soul*, 277
Holy Saturday-Vigil Mass B	*Story of a Soul*, 166–67
Holy Saturday-Vigil Mass C	*Story of a Soul*, 190
Easter Sunday	*The Letters of St. Thérèse*, 2:899

SUGGESTIONS FOR FURTHER READING

ST. THÉRÈSE OF LISIEUX

Ahern, Patrick. *Maurice and Thérèse: The Story of a Love*. New York: Doubleday, 1998.

de Meester, Conrad, O.C.D. *With Empty Hands: The Message of St. Thérèse of Lisieux*. Translated from the French by Mary Seymour. Washington, DC: ICS Publications, 2002.

Egan, Keith J., ed. *Carmelite Prayer: A Tradition for the 21st Century*. Mahwah, NJ: Paulist Press, 2003.

Gaucher, Guy. *The Spiritual Journey of St. Thérèse of Lisieux*. Translated from the French by Sister Anne Marie Brennan, O.D.C. London: Darton, Longman and Todd, 1987.

O'Donnell, Christopher, O.Carm. *Love in the Heart of the Church*. Dublin: Veritas Publications, 1997.

St. Thérèse of Lisieux. *The Letters of St. Thérèse of Lisieux and Those Who Knew Her: General Correspondence (1890–1897)*, vol. 2. Translated from the critical edition by John Clarke, O.C.D. Washington, DC: ICS Publications, 1988. Quotations herein are from this work.

———. *Story of a Soul: The Autobiography of St. Thérèse of Lisieux*. 3rd edition. Translated from the original maniscripts by John Clarke, O.C.D. Washington, DC: ICS Publications, 1996. Quotations herein are this work.

———. *The Poetry of St. Thérèse of Lisieux*. Translated by Donald Kenney, O.C.D. Washington, DC: ICS Publications, 1996. Quotations herein are from this work.

———. *Story of a Soul: Study Edition*. Translated by John Clarke, O.C.D. Prepared by Marc Foley, O.C.D. Washington, DC: ICS Publications, 2005.

———. *The Plays of St. Thérèse of Lisieux: "Pious Recreations."* Translated by Susan Conroy and David Dwyer. Washington, DC: ICS Publications, n.d.

CARMELITE SPIRITUALITY

Slattery, Peter. *The Springs of Carmel: An Introduction to Carmelite Spirituality*. Homebush, NSW: St. Paul Publications, 1990.

Welch, John, O.Carm. *The Carmelite Way*. Mahwah, NJ: Paulist Press, 1996.

INTERNET
RESOURCES

The Order of Carmelites Web site available at
http://www.carmelites.net

ICS Publications Web site available at
http://www.icspublications.org

Christus Publishing, LLC Web site available at
http://www.christuspublishing.com

COVER ART

A detail of the painting, "St. Thérèse of Lisieux" by Leonard Porter, © Leonard Porter 2008, adorns the cover. The painting was commissioned in 2007 by St. Christopher Parish of Staten Island, New York.

Leonard Porter, the artist, was born in 1963, received a Bachelor of Fine Arts from the Rhode Island School of Design in 1986 and a Master of Fine Arts from The School of Visual Arts in 1989. Mr. Porter's work is in public venues and private collections. He resides in New York City where he has a studio. More information about Leonard Porter and his works can be found on his Web site available at www.leonardporter.com.

ABOUT THE
AUTHOR

Fr. John F. Russell, O.Carm. has been a Carmelite friar since 1954. He was ordained to the priesthood in 1960. He earned a Bachelor of Arts degree, majoring in Philosophy, from St. Bonaventure University. Father Russell studied in Rome at Lateran University where he received a Bachelor in Sacred Theology (S.T.B.), and a Licentiate in Sacred Theology (S.T.L.). His first years as a priest were spent in high school ministry, teaching Romance languages. He completed a Master of Arts in educational administration at Roosevelt University in Chicago. He earned his Doctorate in Sacred Theology (S.T.D.) from Catholic University of America in 1979.

Father Russell has had an association with Immaculate Conception Seminary, the graduate school of theology at Seton Hall University in South Orange, New Jersey, for over twenty-two years, teaching Christian Anthropology and a variety of courses in Christian and Carmelite spirituality. He served as the Spiritual Director at Immaculate Conception Seminary from 1995 to 2000. Father Russell was elected. in June, 2002 to serve as the Prior Provincial of the Carmelite Province of the Most Pure Heart of Mary. He served as Provincial until 2005. Presently, he teaches at Immaculate Conception Seminary at Seton Hall University.

In the spring of 2009, Pope Benedict XVI awarded Father Russell the Benemerenti Medal for his exceptional service to the Catholic Church.

He has published chapters in books and articles in such publications as *The Irish Theological Quarterly, Carmelus, Downside Review, Church, Pastoral Life, Studies in Spirituality, Spiritual Life, Review for Religious,* and others. He has cassette programs published by Alba House Communications: "Becoming Spiritually Mature," "A Path to a Contemplative Heart," "A Journey with St. Therese of Lisieux: Doctor of the Church," and "Transforming Nothingness into Fire."